WHAT DO YOU SEE WHEN YOU LOOK IN THE MIRROR?

Also by Nikita Singh

Like a Love Song
Every Time It Rains
Letters to My Ex
The Reason is You

WHAT DO YOU SEE WHEN YOU LOOK IN THE MIRROR?

STORIES

NIKITA SINGH

HarperCollins *Publishers* India

First published in India by
HarperCollins *Publishers* in 2021
A-75, Sector 57, Noida, Uttar Pradesh 201301, India
www.harpercollins.co.in

2 4 6 8 10 9 7 5 3 1

P-ISBN: 978-93-5422-334-1
E-ISBN: 978-93-5422-342-6

Typeset in 11.5/15 Minion Pro at
Manipal Technologies Limited, Manipal

Printed and bound at
Thomson Press (India) Ltd

To Nick, for holding me together.

'The art of a people is a true mirror to their minds.'
– Jawaharlal Nehru

Contents

Author's Note

One of the earliest lessons we are taught in our lives is that of pretence. Because if we don't pretend, if we dare to be ourselves, then *log kya kahenge*? This what-will-people-say question is ingrained in each of our brains to different extents. We all suffer from it. As individuals coexisting in a society, it's inevitable, even natural, to wonder what others think of us. It's when that *wonder* becomes *worry* that we begin to sand down our rough edges to fit the perfectly round mould everyone else seems to inhabit quite effortlessly.

Here's the truth: they don't. It may seem like they do, but no one person is like another. No one person has the exact same emotional, physical or spiritual journey, baggage and struggles as another. And yet, doesn't it always seem like everyone else has their life together? It's because we all want to appear round, like we belong, because rough edges make others uncomfortable.

With this collection, I set out to write stories about people with wildly different perspectives and circumstances, who lead inner lives that would astonish those who presume to know them. My attempt to explore what the inside of these characters' heads looks like is documented in the stories that make up *What Do You See When You Look in the Mirror?*

'Hell is other people,' French philosopher Sartre famously said in his 1944 existentialist play *Huis Clos*. When asked to clarify, he explained, 'If [our] relations with someone else are twisted, vitiated, then that other person can only be hell.'

As if the human condition isn't hard enough, as if it isn't already challenging to love ourselves the way we are, the expectation of others makes it nearly impossible to exist as our truest self. *Hell is other people* because, in a way, we are trapped within other people and the way they view us. We expend precious time trying to change how we are seen, and, in the process, either become masters of pretence or indeed morph into the person we portray.

I have participated in this betrayal. The sides of me you will see if our paths ever crossed – at an airport, or a book tour, or a grocery store, or on social media – those parts don't make a whole. I find it incredibly, debilitatingly challenging to share my grief with others, especially when I'm in the eye of the storm. It's far easier for me to talk about it in retrospect. (This comes from a deep-seated voice buried in my psyche that tells me that secretly, silently, everyone is rooting against me, waiting for me to fail. So, I endure quietly, not giving anyone a chance to relish watching me struggle.)

For instance, 2018 was a terrible year for me. I lost a lot that year: people, places and things. My life was turned upside down. On social media, this translated as inactivity. Apart from sharing information regarding a book tour I went on, I didn't share any other aspect of my life. And 2020, a terrible year for all of us, saw the opposite response from me; I clung to and shared every good moment I experienced. Less frequently, I also shared a digestible version of my struggles. Neither of those years, as presented on social media, provide a complete image of the inside of my head.

This is why I write – to reveal those parts of me I feel secure revealing when it's just you and me. Just some words on paper, and a moment of your devoted attention.

My characters allow me room for honesty, without fear of shame or judgement. In this collection, I am sharing with you the true inner lives of characters who aren't expected to be sensible, to always do the right thing, to spend their lives colouring inside the lines. Because I let them make mistakes, act erratically, do hurtful things, be bad. I allow them terrible thoughts, selfish actions and consequences that can be considered fair or unfair, depending on who you ask.

Apart from the primary theme of secret inner lives, a secondary concept that appears frequently in this collection is the idea that we can't know the impact our words or actions may have on someone else, because we can't know who they are. Even the smallest gesture can hold the biggest meaning for someone. The most insignificant words can shape someone's world, even save someone's life. Perhaps it's worthwhile not to be so careless in our interactions with others. A little kindness can make all the difference (as you'll see in *Talking to Strangers* and *Guru*).

Similarly, stories aren't received the way they are written. I wrote these stories from where I was in my life, and you'll receive them where you are in yours. For me, they range from heart-warming to bizarre. There are themes of love, loss, grief, family, mental health and, of course, society, because those are the kinds of thoughts that have occupied my mind in the past year.

As you read this book, you might have some questions for the person in your mirror. After all of this conditioning, learning and unlearning, what is left of you? Where have you arrived? How much of the person in the mirror is truly you?

Nikita Singh
7 April 2021

Together Forever

'Are you okay?' Sher's worried voice calls from behind her. Preeti moves slightly to the side, revealing the reflection of her husband in the mirror in front of her.

'More than okay. I'm sexy,' she says. She's not lying; she feels sexy. She hasn't felt this way in a long time. She has spent longer than usual in front of the mirror this morning, surveying herself. Her fifty years of life on this planet show in the crevices around her eyes, the wrinkles on the back of her hand, the softness under her skin. While getting dressed this special morning, Preeti had gravitated towards her laciest, most uncomfortable bra. She hadn't worn it in several years, and was pleasantly surprised to find that it still fit perfectly, cupping her breasts in a flattering way. She counted that as a perk of having cancer – the shrinking.

She could now fit into many of her clothes from some time ago, and yet, she didn't have the time, energy or occasion to dress that way. The lehenga choli from Sher's brother's wedding, decades ago, was hardly appropriate for her oncologist appointments.

'Can you be serious for a second?' Sher is especially irritable today. Preeti doesn't take it personally. She senses

1

the worry in his tone, understands the reason behind it. 'You've been … looking at them for a long time. Is everything okay?' he checks.

'*Hey bhagwan!* You can say the word "breasts". You're fifty-five years old! This is the second time your wife has been struck by breast cancer. How are you *still* uncomfortable saying *breasts*?'

'Not everything has to be *mazaak*, okay? I'm just asking you to be serious for one minute. Please?' Sher looks positively pained, and his crumpled face finally wipes the smile off of Preeti's.

'Okay, baba, fine! I'm serious now. Tell me.' She finishes buttoning her silk kurti and turns around to look at him with full attention.

'Come, sit with me.'

Preeti knows what is coming. She takes calculated steps towards him, revising her strategy in her head. She has been expecting this moment, and has a perfect little speech prepared for the occasion. But she'll let him start. She sits down next to him on the bed and places her palm gently on his knee.

'Like Facebook would ask: what's on your mind?' she says, in an attempt to be funny. It lands flat, getting no reaction from Sher, as expected.

'Are you really not scared at all? This is … all very difficult to deal with. I know *I'm* having a hard time …'

'Just don't think about it,' she suggests gently, when in fact, she feels a tide of anger bubbling inside her. They've gone over this already. He needs to stop talking about it, stop letting it occupy his headspace and hers. The rest of

her short life cannot be governed by this stupid cancer. It
has taken too much from her already. Enough is enough.

'I can't just stop thinking about it ...' Sher begins to
complain.

Preeti talks over him loudly, 'We thought about it enough
the first time! That's all we thought about, for two whole
years. I'm done. This is it. Game over. I will *not* let this
cancer take one more moment of our time. It's here, okay?
And it's growing fast. Get that through your thick head.' She
suddenly giggles, poking the side of his head. Lowering her
voice, she adapts that silly, sweet tone they reserve for each
other when no one is watching. 'Are you having second
thoughts or what? You made a promise to me, mister. You
better not back out now!'

'*I'm not backing out.*' Sher speaks like a petulant child
accused of a naughty crime he absolutely did commit.

'*Theek hai fir*, good. Because I don't think you'll make it
without me anyway.' Preeti holds her chin up high in the air.
'*Jo wada kiya woh nibhana padega*,' she sings poorly under
her breath, loud enough for Sher to hear, as she pulls him
close to her. He has to keep his promise. He rests his head
on her shoulder and chuckles.

'What a twisted sense of humour you have, no?'

'Mm-hmm.'

Today is going to be a good day.

❧

Later in the day, they make their way to Chelsea, the posh
neighbourhood in London where their son Ratan lives with

his rapidly growing family. First came Angela, three years ago. They married one year later, had Leo a year after that, and now they're expecting their second baby.

Secretly, Preeti used to wish her sons would be just a little bit on the wild side. Break some rules, stir things up. They didn't move from India to come here, struggle and go on living pretty much the same sheltered, by-the-book lives they would've lived back at home, did they?

Much to her dismay, both her sons were straight arrows. Ratan would have a whole picture-perfect family of four before he turned twenty-eight, later this year. Ronnie, five years younger, was probably on the same beaten path. Preeti prided herself on being a rule-breaker, a cool mom. She never felt part of the tight-knit, talking-behind-each-other's-backs community they had belonged to in India. Being different was important to her. It made her feel special, better than the rest. Just the thought of being one in 7 billion gave her anxiety. She had no other option but to cling to the things about her that were out of the ordinary.

Preeti had lived the first twenty-five years of her life in India and the next twenty-five years in London. During her life in London, she had done everything she wasn't allowed to do back home, followed every instinct, broken every rule that made her unhappy. Even as a twenty-five-year-old small-town Indian woman, flying abroad for the very first time in her life, clutching her three-year-old son's hand, she had felt more thrilled than terrified. It really was a shame that her sons, who received every privilege, every liberty to aim as high as they could, to do whatever in the world their hearts desired, had only ever wanted simple, straightforward lives.

Preeti shakes her thoughts aside and pays attention to little Leo. Angela really did give birth to a perfectly angelic boy. Preeti feels a stab in her chest, not from the cancer, but the knowledge that she would never get to meet the angel Angela currently carried in her swollen belly.

'Gwamma, look!' Leo cries, spotting a waiter carrying a giant cake on a round tray. Preeti spins around to watch. The waiter sets the cake in the middle of the table next to theirs, and lights one of those obnoxious firecracker candles.

'Pwetty,' Leo coos.

'Do you want some ice cream, Leo?' Preeti asks to distract him. The last thing they needed was for the girls on the cake table to offer a toxic residue–covered slice to Leo. 'Ooh, look, Leo, they have chocolate ice cream on the menu. Your favourite! Would you like a scoop of chocolate ice cream?'

Leo is instantly distracted. Angela gives Preeti a grateful look. They both know that if the girls did offer Leo a slice, Ratan probably wouldn't even question the toxins on the cake. His parenting philosophy was rooted in one primary rule: no coddling, which tended to become problematic when he pushed it to an unreasonably dangerous extreme.

'What kind of toppings do you want?' Angela asks Leo in the sweet voice she always reserves for him. Her tone for adults is crisp, sharp, even rude on occasions. Which is why Preeti loves her hot-shot lawyer daughter-in-law so much. Zero times has she seen Angela fake smile to diffuse a situation. Preeti would never say it out loud to her sensitive family, but Angela had earned Preeti's respect in a way her boring sons' attitudes or actions seldom could. Sher would be horrified to hear this truth. He was too sweet, too devoted to their family to ever think of such a thing. It wasn't that Preeti's love for her family wasn't unconditional. It was. But her respect wasn't free.

Preeti elbows Sher's arm for attention. He looks sad. He spins towards her and gives her a wide, fake smile. Was he capable of surviving her death? She wouldn't bet on it. But she had to take action. Her time was here. She couldn't delay it any longer.

She hides it well, but she is in constant pain. Every moment she is awake, every moment she is asleep, she is in pain. Nine days ago, she stopped taking the strong drugs her doctor had prescribed her. Those drugs pushed her deep underwater, leaving her to swim through an impossible pressure pulling her down, trying to drown her. She would cling to familiar bits and pieces, moments of clarity, but before she could save herself, another tide would rise up and swallow her. She didn't want to spend the last days of her life in a state of numbness and disorientation. She wanted to close the book of her life on her own terms.

Everyone chooses how they live. What was so wrong in choosing how they die?

The cancer would take her life anyway, if not today, then tomorrow, or two months from now, maybe three if she was *lucky*. Three months of getting her body cut open, pumped with poison, witnessing the suffering of every person she loved … just like she had the first time around. Only this time, they would not be able to defeat death. Unlike the first time, this time, there is no light at the end of the tunnel. Unacceptable. That's absolutely not the death she deserved. Neither did Sher's wife, Ratan and Ronnie's mother, Leo and the unborn baby's grandmother. She wouldn't force them to watch her die like that.

'I love you, Goose,' she whispers to Sher.

'Love you, Goose,' he says mechanically repeating the nickname they shared. Goose originated from the common term 'silly goose' and they used it when the other was being silly, or they wanted some silliness. Sher is distracted by the new arrival: Ronnie is standing in front of them, holding the hand of a man roughly the same age and same build as him. Both of them are 5'10" with meticulously groomed beards, shirts buttoned all the way up, shining eyes.

'*Chalo, badhiya hai!* Perfect!' Preeti cheers, clapping her hands together.

'Maa …' Ronnie looks uncertainly from her to Sher, as if his silly old parents don't understand. 'Kevin is my boyfriend.'

'Hi, Kevin,' Preeti says, smiling her biggest smile of the day so far. 'How do you do?'

'I'm gay!' Ronnie cries out, frustrated by the tepid response of his family to this bomb he has just dropped.

'Good for you, bro,' Ratan says.

'Adds up.' Angela nods thoughtfully.

'Are you sure?' Sher asks meekly, but Preeti shushes him.

'Oh, *aap bhi na!* Come on!' She slaps his back softly and turns back to her younger son, her baby boy. 'I'm not backward like your father. I know all about this stuff. I love you, trust you, respect your choices and I am proud of you!' she says, sounding quite proud of herself.

'Really? Are you really okay with this?' Ronnie asks eagerly. Poor boy; he must've held his truth so close to his heart for so long.

'Yes! It's your life, your time on the planet. Be who makes you happy.' Ronnie runs to her then and picks her up in a giant hug. For a moment, he feels like her little boy Ronit again, before he turned thirteen, towered over her and announced in a newly developed deep voice that he was to be referred to as Ronnie henceforth. As her younger son smothers her, Preeti holds out a hand for her older son to join them. Ratan brings Leo. Sher and Angela exchange a look, and join the group hug. Kevin stands awkwardly, watching this family drama go down.

Preeti beams, overjoyed with the knowledge that she had the chance to give her son this gift of acceptance, and share this perfect final moment with her family before she went home and ended her life.

❦

Soon afterwards, they drive away from the expensive part of London their sons preferred, to their home in the Indian part of London. Preeti looks outside the window, saying goodbye to the streets, the grey sky, the hum of the city she has called home for half her life. There's beauty in the way she has lived her life, a symmetry she appreciates.

It's her time to go. But not before she shares herself with her husband one last time. They make love unhurriedly, forgetting about what's coming, their chests rising and falling in the present. All we can ever dare to ask for are moments. And this, here, is another beautiful moment they are fortunate enough to share.

❦

Preeti gets dressed, carefully, one last time. She will be found like this, wearing her favourite green salwar kurti. She's ready. She has written letters to her sons, explaining, thanking them, saying goodbye. She walks around the house, peeks inside every room, takes her time. Then, she makes the bed, perfectly, every layer exactly where it should be. She stands at the foot of the bed and looks at it. This bed was one of the first things they had bought when she had moved to London. A three-year-old Ratan had slept between Sher and Preeti on nights when he was too scared to be alone in this foreign house. Some years later, Ronit had done the same.

Preeti feels a sob rise in her chest. She lets it out. She allows herself a moment to wallow in the injustice of her life having been cut short. She was getting pushed off the train, even though the station she had planned to disembark on was miles away. The train will keep moving forward, carrying everyone she loves, without her.

Eventually, she sniffs, wipes her face and pulls off the covers. She slides in.

Sher stands at the foot of the bed and watches, tears trickling down his face, getting trapped in his big, grey moustache. The trembling of his brows as he tries and fails to contain the emotions bubbling inside him trigger a wave of sorrow in Preeti. He's wearing a white kurta pyjama. He looks just as handsome as he did all those years ago, when Preeti celebrated her first Holi with her new husband. She lets the tears travel down her face unchecked.

'Shera,' she breathes. Another private nickname, the oldest one. Preeti holds up two small plastic bottles of what she refers to as "cocktails" to Sher – filled with exactly the mix of ingredients they each need for their hearts to stop beating. She pats his side of the bed, inviting him.

He follows her lead. Slides under the covers, turns towards her and cradles her head in the crevice of his arm. She can hear his heart beat manically in his chest.

The decision to die together isn't one they had taken lightly, or recently. Preeti's parents had fought together for India's freedom. They had met very young, revolted against the British together, and tied the knot after India reclaimed her Independence. They had endured sixteen heartbreaking years of miscarriages and crushed hopes before they had Preeti. Her parents were in their late-thirties then, and had already lived through more tragedies than many people face in their lifetime. Preeti was in her early twenties when her father passed away of a cardiac arrest. Her mother aged ten years overnight. She aged thirty more years in the three years she lived after her husband's passing. She was present at Preeti's wedding and the birth of her first grandchild.

She passed soon after, of an accumulation of accelerated natural causes. She simply didn't know how to be without her husband. They were halves of a whole. Without him, she could exist, but never be happy. She died of heartbreak.

Soon after her death, Sher moved Preeti and Ratan to London. Sher had already been living and working there for two years by then. His responsibility was to earn money and send it home to his family, while hers was to care for her dying mother. When her mother passed, Preeti had arrived in London, crumpled and raw, and told Sher earnestly that if something were to happen to him, she wouldn't survive it. Then, seeing how Preeti's mother suffered, the pain she had been in ever since her husband died, Sher had told Preeti that he couldn't survive her loss either. That's when they had promised that they would die together.

Over the following year, they had discussed the logistics. Ratan would need a sibling. Both children would need to have grown up, moved out and on their feet. Once those non-negotiable requirements were fulfilled, if anything happened to either of them, the other would leave too. They would go together. Neither could live with the image of the other person suffering their loss. It's easier for those who die. Death affects those who live.

Preeti speaks slowly. 'You have given me everything I ever needed in my time on this planet. I love you, and our family, with everything I have. I know you think I'm eager to leave. I'm really not. My body is failing me. It's my time, Shera. This is how it ends, and I wouldn't have it any other way.'

'I love you, Preet,' Sher says in his brave, broken voice.

'Thank you for keeping your promise. I asked everything of you, and you gave it to me. You gave me a forever.' Preeti sobs into Sher's chest, breathing in his scent. Her fingers run over his body, basking in his warmth and familiarity.

'Together forever,' he murmurs into her hair.

'Together forever,' Preeti repeats their promise.

They lie there for a while. Exactly how long, neither of them knows. When they're ready, they sit up. Preeti hands Sher a red bottle, containing a small, round red tablet and a large white one. She unscrews the blue bottle, containing an assortment of four tablets and capsules. She transfers all four of them into her palm, reaches for the bottle of water on the nightstand and looks at Sher. He's in the ready position too, just like her.

They kiss. They pull away. She looks her husband in the eyes, swallows her cocktail. She slips back under the covers, adjusts herself on the pillow and waits. A moment later, Sher takes position next to her.

Their book ends here. She murmurs to him, sweetly, softly. Whispers loving memories into his ears, till she can't anymore. She feels at peace. Her heart slows down. The blood in her veins relax; they're not in a rush anymore. She is prepared for this. This is exactly the way she planned it. Peaceful, quiet, in her husband's arms.

This is the way for her.

❦

Preeti slips back into consciousness at the sound of his words.

'Mmm?' she manages to groan.

'I'm sorry,' Sher's voice reaches her as though from the other side of a door. It grows clearer. 'I couldn't do it. I couldn't take my cocktail. I'm sorry.'

She hears him, loud and clear. Her heart races one last time.

'I'm sorry … I'm so sorry …'

Before she can retaliate in any way, she is gone, not in the way she'd planned it.

🌹

Sher sits up in bed. He is stunned. He watches the limp body of his wife. Her eyes are hollow, looking up at the ceiling. He feels too weak to shut her frozen eyelids. Too weak to even look at her.

He turns away, looks at the two tablets, still in the bottle, *his* bottle. He doesn't know what they are. Preeti had done the research, told him to trust her. Their bodies were different, needed different things to live, different things to die. He had left the job of finding the perfect cocktail to end his life to her.

For a moment, he feels a sudden compulsion to take his cocktail now, leave with her after all. Then, he hardens himself. *This isn't betrayal.* Her time was up, his isn't. He couldn't have told her that and broken their promise. He would've made her last days on earth miserable. And he knew she wouldn't change her mind. For as long as he'd known her, she had held this promise close to her heart. It had meant so much to her. It wasn't only important, it was non-negotiable.

So, he had decided to let her go quietly. Grant half of her wish. *This isn't betrayal.* Anyone would tell you that it's completely unreasonable to expect someone else to die with you just because you were cursed with a terminal disease that will eventually kill you.

Watching her go, however, he hadn't been able to keep the truth from her any longer. In a moment of weakness, he'd revealed his betrayal. *This isn't betrayal.* Then why did it feel so much like it?

🌹

Eventually, he does gather enough courage to look at her, shut her eyelids. Eventually, he does call his sons, the ambulance. After he had apologized to his wife's dead body a hundred more times.

This isn't fair to him. He should've had the liberty to grieve his wife without feeling like a fraud. She took that from him. Now, he doesn't know what to think, what to do with his life.

❧

In the days and weeks that follow, Sher finds a way to cope the only way he can: by not thinking about Preeti's death. He plays pretend with himself. Not in a delusional way, but in a forced, only-way-to-survive way. He convinces himself that she is away, visiting a friend. That she will return someday soon.

While she is gone, he focuses on all the things her presence limited in his life. He goes home, to his village. He stays up all night with his friends, whom Preeti had considered a bit uncouth. Spending nights around a bonfire, talking noisily about the memories of their horseplay in their childhood, Sher feels a sense of triumph.

A month later, when he returns to their home in London, that feeling dictates his mindset. He revels in his new-found freedom. There was a lot he couldn't do because she disliked it or was simply uninterested. He focuses on those things. He never goes on the morning jogs Preeti forced on him. He orders food she didn't like, watches movies she wasn't a fan of, listens to old Punjabi folk music on speakers throughout the house. He buys more underwear to put off doing laundry longer; he buys the plants she was allergic to; he throws all the cushions on the floor to make more room on the couch and leaves the curtains drawn all day. He tells himself that it's not because he wants to hide from the world. It's because he's finally comfortable in his own home.

He doesn't pay heed to her absence, or the things she left behind. On the day he returned from India, he had brought out a pillow and a blanket from the guest room to the living room, where he sleeps on the couch every night.

Time passes slowly. Days blend into each other, with nothing to tell them apart. He doesn't venture into the bedroom. He knows that there are letters waiting for their sons, in the closet next to their clothes. Preeti had taken some time to meticulously collect their personal belongings from all around the house and pile them together in a corner in their bedroom. She didn't want to leave that job to their sons. She had donated whatever could be donated, piled up the rest in their bedroom, leaving behind only furniture and furnishings in the rest of the house. The house felt like a bed and breakfast. Warm and comfortable, but lacking in personal effects: photographs, memorabilia from their travels, small things of sentimental value to them but useless junk to strangers, clothes, jewellery and such.

Two months after his wife took her life, Sher still hasn't gone into their bedroom.

Three months since the day Preeti took her cocktail and he didn't take his, Sher still finds himself carrying the small plastic bottle with him, for reasons unknown to him.

Sher doesn't want to spend the day alone. Ratan and Angela are only too glad to have him babysit Leo while they spend the day looking at bigger apartments in preparation for the new baby. Sher appreciates Leo's bright and energetic company. His grandson occupies his mind, his giggles bring joy to Sher's heart. At times, Sher laughs so hard, tears threaten to emerge from where he has hidden them.

Things change so suddenly, so drastically, that it knocks the breath out of Sher's body. Leo is on the floor. His small body is convulsing.

For one panic-stricken moment, Sher is petrified. Frozen to the spot, unable to move, do anything but watch his grandson tremble violently. It takes everything Sher has in him to move. With superhuman energy, he rushes to find a phone, dials 999. Cradling the mobile phone between his shoulder and ear, he runs back to Leo, drops to the floor on his knees and lifts his grandson in his arms. He gives the operator clear, concise instructions. Once he's assured that the ambulance has been dispatched, Sher hangs up the call and stands up, carrying Leo with him. The boy doesn't cry. His body shakes and shivers, but Leo is missing. His body feels like a shell.

'It's okay, it's okay, shh. You're okay, you're okay,' Sher chants like a prayer.

Leo's body is burning. His little face is inflamed. The spittle on the corners of his lips terrifies Sher. He sits Leo down again and helps him throw up. He pats his back first and then rubs it frantically.

'No, no, no, Leo, please, no,' he begs and pleads his grandson to be okay. 'What did you do? What did you do?'

The ambulance arrives within minutes. They don't waste any time collecting Leo and securing him in.

'Are you coming, sir?' the paramedic asks Sher, who is frozen again now that someone else has the reins. He's jolted into action. He nods and climbs into the ambulance. Someone shuts the doors. Someone else drives them away. Time flies by.

The paramedics say things Sher can't grasp. He crouches next to Leo, brushes his damp hair away from his forehead, whispers assurances that everything will be okay. He doesn't know that. He doesn't know anything. What was in the cocktail Preeti had customized for him? Would it have the same effects on Leo that it would've had on Sher? Why did Sher carry the deadly cocktail with him? How did Leo's little arms reach the inside pockets of Sher's jacket, which he had hung on the coat rack? Had it fallen to the floor? Why did Sher look away, even for one second? If something bad happened, would Ratan and Angela survive it? Would their marriage survive? Would Ratan ever be okay, after losing his mother and son so close together? A hundred questions swirl in Sher's mind. He doesn't have any answers.

They arrive at the hospital. Leo is carried away. Sher runs behind him till he is stopped. He calls Ratan. He paces the waiting room. His entire body is dry. There's nothing left there. It's like there's no blood flowing in his veins, like he has no tears left. His mouth feels like sandpaper. He looks up to see Ratan and Angela approach. He sees them see him. He can't hold the pieces of himself together anymore. He turns away. He starts walking. He keeps walking.

🌹

Sher falls to the floor. He's in the bedroom. He's furious with Preeti.

'What did you do? What the hell did you do?' he screams in agony.

In the dark, cold bedroom, he rifles through the boxes, searching for something to hold on to, something to stop his free fall. He looks around himself. He wants to rip the hair off his head, gouge his eyes out of their sockets. He has forgotten his jacket at Ratan's house, and yet, his body is hot. He's sweating through his shirt, and yet, the tips of his fingers are freezing as he digs through Preeti's belongings.

He finds the stack of letters. There are three sets. One set of about a dozen letters is gathered and held together by a rubber band. It's addressed to Ratan. A second set is addressed to Ronnie. There's a third set. For Angela? He didn't realize that Preeti was that close to Angela. No. It's not addressed to Angela. It's addressed to him.

My Dear Shera, My Love, the bundle reads, in Preeti's handwriting.

With trembling fingers, Sher peels open the first letter. His first few attempts to read end in failure. He blinks rapidly, shakes his head, as if to force it to operate correctly. He tries again.

I know this is confusing. It wasn't easy for me either.

I knew the part after I take my cocktail and die would be the hardest for you, since your cocktail was just a ferrous sulphate and a Vitamin C tablet. Iron and vitamin supplements, that's all. So, you must have had to watch me go. That could not have been easy.

Sher's phone rings, and he starts. He picks up the call, without meaning to. He doesn't say anything. His voice doesn't work.

'Papa, everything's okay! Leo is okay! It's a peanut allergy. We didn't know about it. The doctor said your fast response saved his life. He said that – Papa? Are you there?'

The phone slips from Sher's hand, on to the floor. His body follows. He curls up with his dead wife's letters. Relief rushes through his veins, for Leo. Misery, for Preeti. He betrayed her. She didn't betray him.

He reads on.

I'm sorry, Shera, but I didn't have any other choice. I couldn't have told you that it was my time, but not yours. You would never have let me go. And I didn't want to let you die either. You have reasons to live. Our children, Leo, your job, your friends, your book club, a second grandchild on the way.

We had a full lifetime together. My chapter needed to end. But you still have so much more steam. I couldn't let you give that away. You have so much more life left in you. Thirty more years, easily. Probably even forty or fifty, if you're really good with food and keep up the morning jogs.

He can't read anymore. For the first time since she left, Sher lets himself think about her. The real her, not the version he had conjured up in his head as a coping mechanism, highlighting her small flaws and quirks to villainize her. It had been easier that way. But he doesn't have that comfort anymore. He can't hide behind his constructed hatred.

He feels the grief of losing her. Really feels it.

He betrayed her trust. Not only that, he didn't trust her either. He let her die with the knowledge of his betrayal. He was finally shaken out of his insulated blanket, his false sense of security today, when he thought Leo was dying because of him, because of her. When, all along, she had been looking out for him.

He clutches her letters to his heart. Would he ever be strong enough to read them?

🌹

He has to grant Preeti her wishes. He has to live the life she had saved for him. His punishment is to live that life, but without her. His life partner, his secret-keeper, his companion.

He spends a long time on the floor like that. He thinks about her, about what he has done. When he can't contain anymore thoughts, he falls back to reliving memories. There, he finds pain. There, he finds solace.

They had made enough memories to last him the rest of his life. He talks to her. He feels her presence around him. He asks her what she thinks about what he did.

He can picture her vividly. She chuckles. Says, 'You bad, *bad* man! You backstabber, you!' She laughs some more. Then she adds, begrudgingly, 'I must admit that I'm quite impressed with you. Didn't think you had it in you to do something so bad. All this time, I thought you were a good boy.'

He can almost see her wink. He clings to it. Clings to her memories. He follows her wish. He goes on, with some help from her letters.

Sellout

In a matter of minutes, Parul's day had spiralled wildly out of control. The family's carefully structured routine had failed to bring the organization to their schedules that Parul, her husband and their two daughters relied on. It looked like it was up to Parul to fix it.

She thought back to the series of events that led them to this place. The previous night, Parul had helped both her daughters prepare for their class test, and still, miraculously, gone to bed on time and woken up fully rested. This morning, a sort of domino effect had played out in the Mehra household. When she woke up, her husband was still asleep, which was unusual for him, since his office hours started two hours before hers. She tried to wake him up, only being successful in extracting a moan from him as he begged for five more minutes of sleep.

She went down to the kitchen, packed lunch boxes for her daughters, wished them both good luck for their tests and sent them off to catch the school bus. Six minutes later, the doorbell rang furiously. Parul picked up her clothes from where they lay on the bathroom floor and hurriedly put them back on.

'Mayank, come on, wake up,' she hollered, as she slid out of the bathroom to rush towards the sound of their daughters, who were outside the front door, screaming frantically for their father. On her way out, Parul put on sneakers and checked her reflection in the mirror. Her hair was big and wild. She wrapped a scarf around her head to bring some order to her hair and also cover her sleep T-shirt.

'It's okay, it's okay,' Parul said, swinging the front door open, stepping out and locking it behind her. She rubbed away the crusts collected at the corners of her eyes and put on sunglasses. She placed both her hands on her daughters' backs and led them out to the car. 'I'll drive you to your school. Let's go.'

'Where's Papa?' Maya, the eight-year-old, questioned.

'Still asleep. How did you miss the bus?'

Her daughters screamed over each other in response. One blamed the other for stopping to pick a flower for her teacher, and the other blamed the first for not running fast enough when she saw that the bus was leaving.

'I'm smaller than you! My legs are smaller than yours!' Jiya, the six-year-old, moaned.

'Why didn't you think about that before stopping to get that stupid flower?'

'My flower is *not* stupid. It's for Miss Kavita!'

'Ooh, your favourite Miss Kavita! Why are you so obsessed with her? Everybody calls you a teacher's pet …'

Parul let them argue. It was good for them. They didn't need to get along with each other, not yet, but they needed to talk to each other, and if the only way her daughters could communicate with each other was through foolish arguments, so be it. Mayank was an only child, so he didn't understand (he had asked on many occasions, horrified, 'Is this normal?' and Parul assured him each time that it was as normal as two sisters that age could get), but Parul knew that it took a significant amount of time for sisters to become friends.

'Okay, here we are. Feel ready for your tests?'

'Yes, Mumma,' Jiya said in her sweet voice.

'*Yes, Mumma,*' Maya imitated sarcastically.

'Don't copy me!'

'*Don't copy me!*'

'Please, stop!'

'*Please, stop!*'

Maya's tone was getting whinier with every word. By the time her daughters got out of the car, Parul had stopped listening, intentionally ignoring bad behaviour. Her attention would only further encourage said behaviour to occur again. Patting herself on the back for her smart parenting decisions, she drove back home.

At home, she peeked into the kitchen and the bathroom before going into the bedroom. The curtains were still drawn, leaving the room dark.

'Mayank?' she breathed softly. He was still in bed. His thick black hair was matted, sticking to his face as he lay on his stomach with his face to the side. Parul pushed his hair out of the way. Before she reached for his forehead, she already knew he was sick. He was such a bright morning person that it would take something significant to keep him in bed.

'How do you feel?' she whispered, lowering herself on the floor next to him.

'Crappy,' Mayank groaned.

'Where does it hurt?'

'Everywhere ...'

'Can you be a little more specific so that I can try to help you?'

'Head and stomach, and throat. And nose and eyes.'

Parul ran her fingers through his damp hair, gently massaging his scalp. She was smiling; her husband was a very self-sufficient, able person. He barely ever needed anyone's help with anything. So, on rare occasions, when he behaved like a child, it was endearing to her.

Parul worked from home, as a freelance book editor, so it would be easy enough for her to make sure that Mayank was cared for. But she might need to move her meetings and reschedule her appointment with a new author. While she mentally recalibrated her calendar, her phone rang. She got up to walk to the sound of the phone, which was coming from her handbag in the living room. It was an unknown number, calling on her business phone number. She picked it up, expecting an editorial query.

'Hi, this is Parul Mehra.'

'Hi, Parul, I'm calling from The Lowdown. We're a multi-media entertainment company. You can find us on YouTube and pretty much everywhere on social media. I have a question for you.'

'Yes?' Parul said warily.

'A proposition, really. Would you be interested in giving us the dirt on the *real* Akanksha Seth? As you must know, she's under fire, after the recent exposé last week. We're looking for more information about who she really is, from a reliable source such as you, her very own sister.'

Parul was stunned into silence.

'Of course, we will pay you and make sure our source remains anonymous. As long as you can give us some shady drama, we can make you rich.'

Parul's jaw hardened with disgust. At this disgrace of a reporter, at her past life that she had worked so hard to forget. Through clenched teeth, she declared, 'Akanksha Seth is not my sister.'

She peeled the phone from her ear with trembling fingers, and before she touched the red circle to end the call, she heard a faint 'think about it' from the other end.

There's nothing to think about. She collected herself. She was already behind schedule for a meeting, had a sick husband to look after, and an entire day's work waiting for her.

❦

As the day went on, it turned out that there was a lot to think about. In fact, no matter how hard she tried, Parul couldn't stop thinking about it.

She caught up on the 'drama' around Akki circulating on the internet. She felt even more disgusted with the guy from

The Lowdown after reading the articles. From what Parul could find, this was a very serious matter. The fact that he had referred to it as 'drama' and used words like 'dirt', 'exposé' and 'shady' had made it sound juvenile.

Parul forced herself to put it out of her mind. She focused on work instead. It was only after she had finished everything that absolutely needed to be done that day and staggered the rest of her work to other days of the week, that she shut her laptop screen and pushed her chair back.

Leaning against the bedroom door, she said, 'Remember Akki? I told you about her?'

'Hmm?' her husband mumbled in his sleep. She had given him a tablet for his headache a few hours ago.

'Are you asleep? I need to talk to you about something. It's serious,' she said gently, climbing on to the bed next to him.

'We should just go for it. Just do it. Get married,' Mayank blurted out, suddenly springing to attention.

His delirious, sleepy nonsense triggered an involuntary sob from Parul. 'We got married already, love. We've been married for ten years,' she said through happy tears. She had a perfect life. Not perfect for everyone, but perfect for her … It was all she needed. A family of people who truly loved each other. Her job essentially involved her reading books and working with brilliant authors to make their work even better, and, sometimes, her daughters got along with each other as well.

Mayank was fully alert now. Still lying down, he asked, 'What time is it?'

'It's almost five. The kids are outside, playing. I finished work and came to check on you. How are you feeling?' She touched his forehead with the back of her hand. 'Still warm.'

'A little better,' Mayank said. 'Did I just propose to you?'

'I wouldn't call it a proposal, per se. You did suggest we get married though.'

They laughed. In the pause that followed, Parul's mind wandered back to the phone call from earlier. 'Something weird happened ...' she began, unsure about how deep she wanted to go into it. 'I got a phone call from a trashy YouTube channel looking for dirt on Akki.'

'Your soul sister?' Mayank asked. His tone was light, but his body had become still, and his eyes were searching hers. He knew this was serious.

'It's so bizarre,' Parul said. 'A decade after everything ended, randomly, I get this call ... And it's so disgusting too. Something terrible happened to her, and they just want ammo to throw at her ...'

'I actually read about it,' Mayank said softly, surprising her. 'A few days ago. A news article popped up for me. I didn't say anything to you, because I thought that's what you would want.'

Parul nodded. She had taken that strategy with everything related to Akki, since their fallout. But this ... this she couldn't ignore. If she had ever been her friend, she needed to do something, say something. 'I'm going to talk to her.'

'I think that's for the best,' Mayank said, surprising her again. Historically, Mayank had stayed firmly out of anything that had to do with Parul's relationship with Akanksha.

'Really?'

'Yes, I didn't want to say anything, but if you ask me, I think you should talk to her.'

Parul nodded. Her heart raced at the thought of reaching out to Akki. Ten years had passed since they had last communicated. So much had happened in that time. Their lives had taken such different directions. She wasn't even the same person anymore, and neither was Akki, judging by her social media presence.

She sat still next to Mayank for a long time, only her chest rising and falling. He didn't say anything else. Yet, she could sense his quiet support, and appreciation for the fact that she would need some time to gather herself, her thoughts and her memories, before taking any kind of action.

The kids came home from school soon after, giving Parul a valid distraction. She got busy with their evening routine – homework, TV, shower, bedtime story – and by the time she came back to the bedroom with Mayank's dinner, she was itching to talk to Akanksha. It was strange how something she had dreaded so much the first time she thought about it had morphed into something she longed to do, all in the course of a day.

Mayank nibbled on his khichdi, clearly struggling to keep it down. He hadn't been able to eat much all day. 'You're such a baby,' she said, shaking her head.

'I know you crushed gobhi and sneaked it in here. I can taste the cauliflower!' Mayank pretend-gagged.

'No, I didn't! I know you hate gobhi, so why would I force-feed it to you?' Parul lied through her teeth.

'Okay, I believe you,' Mayank said. His narrowed eyes, clearly indicating that he didn't believe her one bit.

'Thank you.'

That light-hearted moment between them loosened the knot inside Parul just enough for her to open her mailbox and type a quick email. Last she heard, Akki was living in Dubai; the chances of her still using her old phone number were slim.

'I did it. I emailed her. Just a short message asking how she's doing—' Parul was cut off by her phone ringing. Unlike Akki, Parul was still using the same phone number. Without even looking down at her screen which flashed an unknown number, Parul knew it was Akki.

'Take it,' Mayank said, encouragingly.

Parul gulped, but her throat was dry. She wasn't ready for this. She couldn't do this. Panic rose inside her chest and she succumbed to it. She let the phone ring, till it stopped ringing. She was breathing hard. She didn't want to go back to that time and relive the heartache. It had taken her years to overcome it. A decade, a full decade.

Mayank pulled her into a hug. 'It's okay. There's no rush.' His handsome face looked at her with concern. A five o' clock shadow had appeared, just from one day of skipping shaving, making him even more handsome than usual. He smelled of sweat and deodorant. Parul frowned at her ill-timed arousal. In the next moment, she suddenly felt ready.

'I'm calling her back,' she announced, rising from the bed. Before Mayank had the chance to react, she had already left the room. She had momentum now, thanks to the roller coaster of emotions she was feeling, so she kept going. She called back the number and held her phone to her ear. The call rang one and a half times before it was picked up.

'Parul!' a voice Parul didn't recognize, said.

'Hello?' Parul spoke tentatively. It probably wasn't even her. All of this anxiety had been for nothing.

'Parul, it's me. I got your email. How are you?'

It *was* her. Her voice sounded different. Deeper, as if she had a cold. Or she now spoke from the back of her throat. 'Akki, thanks for calling me,' Parul said stiffly. She immediately questioned her tone and her choice of words.

'Thank *you* for reaching out! I was so glad to get your email.' Akki's tone sounded so earnest, it knocked the breath out of Parul. She sounded so genuine. So happy, and so sad.

The walls around Parul came down. 'I … I had to. I got this call from … some losers. Are you okay …?' Parul's face distorted with the last few words. Tears flowed out of her eyes and freely down her cheeks. That question. That small, seemingly insignificant everyday-sounding question felt so good to finally say out loud. Parul had wanted to ask her friend that for so long, so many times through the years.

Parul heard an unmistakable sob at the other end. Her hand went to her mouth and she sniffed. They cried on the phone, without saying anything. The tears didn't seem to stop. So much emotion had been lying stagnant within her for so long. And this news … it put everything in perspective. So much of what happened all those years ago became clear. While, at the same time, recent events also raised a myriad questions.

A few minutes later, Parul gathered herself enough to ask the most pressing one, 'Why didn't you tell me?'

'I couldn't! He didn't let me. You have no idea, Parul. I was his prisoner. He used to whisper threats to me, late at night, when I pretended to be asleep. He used to tell me what he would do to me if I told anyone. You don't know how dangerous he is—'

'I could've helped you! If only you had—'

'You couldn't have! You don't know! He said he would hurt you, and I knew his threats weren't empty. He used to hurt me where no one could see. He was so strategic, so calculated. He thought out everything beforehand … He literally had me in his web. I didn't have a chance—'

'You should've said something—'

'Pari, you don't understand. You had to be there to understand what I went—'

'I *was* there. I was there with you, till you pushed me out of your life!'

'I had to—'

'Why? There had to have been another way! A better way!' Parul's voice was hoarse with hysteria.

Akki's voice was louder, drowning out everything Parul said. 'There wasn't, not without putting you in danger. If you pay attention to what's happening now, it's so clear that he's winning, and he would've won back then! No one believes me! They don't believe me now and they wouldn't have believed me then!'

Parul took that in. Akki was right. She paused to think, her mind racing in all directions. What could she do? She so desperately wanted to help her friend. Her thoughts ran wild. She couldn't find the head or tail of anything. Completely overwhelmed, she sat down on the couch, and reflected on everything she thought had happened ten years ago, in light of what Akki was telling her now.

Parul and Akki had grown up together. They'd met in second grade and remained close throughout school. They considered each other their soul sister. It wasn't a coincidence that they had ended up in the same college. Their relationship was special, their banter with each other fascinating, even to others. They'd heard people say that enough number of times to fully believe it and start a bi-weekly podcast together.

They grew at a pace that shocked them. In their first year, they already had sponsorships. In their second year, they had national brand deals. In the third year, they had to hire a team to help them, and, by the fourth year, they were flying in guests on a weekly basis. They talked about topics they were passionate about, things everyone in their generation was dealing with, conversations that were considered taboo topics, or *bold* – and they did it in an approachable way. They talked about self-love, mental health, body-shaming, cat-calling, patriarchy, gender, sexual orientation, the climate crisis, overconsumption, capitalism, sexual health and modern relationships – and they did it in a raw, honest way. People across the country tuned in, pulled in by the hosts' candour and sensitivity.

In their fifth year, which ended up becoming their last, things took a turn. Akki began dating someone. Dev seemed nice to Parul, a little snobbish maybe. In a strange way, his presence in their lives highlighted the differences between Parul and Akki. Akki was clearly the more glamourous one; she was gorgeous, tall with stylish, short hair, piercing dark eyes and a quirky fashion sense. When Akki entered a room, heads turned and strangers paid attention. Parul, on the other hand, was beautiful in an understated kind of way, not nearly as outgoing as Akki. She was funny and thoughtful, easily obsessed with new discoveries. They were both deeply passionate, but exhibited it in very different ways, one more approachable than the other.

Dev began questioning things Parul and Akki had never had reason to question. What was Parul's plan after graduation? Why wasn't Parul as ambitious as Akki? Why didn't Parul hire a stylist? Was Parul holding Akki back? Over the course of a year, these small, seemingly unrelated questions settled somewhere deep under Parul's skin. It was clear to her that she was getting in the way of the stardom Akki was surely headed towards. When they wrapped up the fifth season of their podcast, they didn't talk about ending it. They also didn't talk about returning for another season.

Parul tried to reach out to Akki a few times. Akki always seemed to have something urgent or important going on. If, by some miracle, she did have an opening on her calendar, Dev always accompanied her.

Their fallout wasn't dramatic at all. On her birthday, Parul received a text message from Akki apologizing for not seeing her party invite on time and informing Parul that she was going to be out of town. Parul didn't point out that her boyfriend, Dev, had already declined her invitation as soon as she had sent it out. Parul told Akki to reach out when she got back and had time. Akki promised that she would … and never did.

To Parul, it felt like she had lost someone she loved, it hurt so much. Grief engulfed her. For years, Parul truly believed that Akki was too good for her. That Akki was the star, and Parul was her crutch. She had to let her go. And the fact that Akki removed Parul from her life so swiftly, without a second thought, after being closer than sisters for all of their lives, hurt like a dagger to her heart.

It took Parul years to recover from that rejection. She hated Dev at first, but that didn't last long. He was insignificant. He had only played a role in revealing what Akki must always have thought of Parul. She had always felt this way, Parul was sure.

She watched Akki's social media presence explode. In the years that followed the end of their podcast, Akki grew a fan base on Instagram, producing high-quality lifestyle content: from travel to food to fashion to beauty. Her content also reflected her intelligence. She wrote compelling captions about cyberbullying, body-shaming, mental health and everything else they used to talk about on their podcast – in fewer words, to a far larger audience.

After a while, Parul muted Akki's accounts, so to anyone who cared to check, it looked like she still followed her former business partner. This way, she could keep up pretences, but, by muting her, she no longer had to follow what Akki was doing anymore. That was the only way to move on with her life.

Without the podcast, Parul mourned the lack of an outlet for her thoughts. It really affected her mental health. Desperate for stimulation, she joined a publishing house as an editor. She worked there for three years, and built a strong reputation in the industry for her keen editorial eye. Eventually, Parul left the company and started her own independent editorial company, which allowed her far more freedom to choose her clients and projects – authors she admired and really wanted to work with.

Shortly after that, she met Mayank and started her family, leaving behind the pain from her past life and her abandonment issues. Secretly, she also began work on her dream project: writing a book.

The news of Akki's break-up with Dev reached her through the grapevine. Occasionally, Parul would see Akki's photos, feel a pang of nostalgia, followed by a heaviness in her chest, prompting her to scroll away. It was only this morning, after the phone call, that she had searched Akki's name on the internet, and read every piece of information that was available.

One week ago, Akki had done an exclusive interview with a mainstream magazine, opening up about continuous physical, mental and sexual abuse at the hands of her ex-boyfriend. Dev had responded immediately with an attack on her, claiming that she had absolutely no proof of these false accusations. He claimed that she was doing this for clout. Dev had leaked phone conversations between him and their old podcast employees, in which the employees called Akki a 'controlling bitch'. Finally, Dev had concluded that if Akki's allegations were true, why didn't Parul intervene? After all, wasn't Parul the person who had known Akki the longest? He questioned why her own best friend, soul sister, didn't even talk to her, if not for the reason that Akki was a manipulative, attention-seeking bitch.

The internet turned on Akki in a second. Her haters camouflaging as her followers had a field day. Hashtags like #ibelievehim began trending on Twitter, with thousands of people showing their support for Dev. Disgusting drama channels on YouTube released a series of videos based on 'information' from anonymous 'reliable sources' close to the parties involved. The media and the public jumped on the opportunity to attack a beautiful, successful, self-sufficient woman, based on retaliation from her abuser and pure conjecture.

'I can't believe this …' Parul whispered, shaking her head frantically from side to side. How did this happen? How did she not see this? She was right there; this had happened right under her nose.

'I'm not a liar! It did happen! I wouldn't make something like this up for—'

'I know, I know, I know,' Parul rushed to explain, talking over Akki. 'I believe you. Of course, I believe you, Akki. I believe you.'

Akki went quiet.

'I just can't believe that I didn't see this … It was right in front of me.'

'I hid it pretty well. But I can't take all the credit for that. Any time I let the mask slip, I would be punished later.'

'What a psychopathic piece of shit!' Parul spat. 'He won't get away with this, Akki. Trust me, we won't let him get away with this.'

'He's already gotten away with it. No one believes me.'

'They will believe you! These people have followed you for years. If we lead them to the truth, in the right direction, they will—'

'No, no, no.' Parul could picture Akki shaking her head in resignation. 'So many of them have followed me for years just waiting for a chance to pounce. They've cancelled me. You don't know how this world works. It's been a long time since we used to do the podcast together … It's not the same audience.' Akki's voice lowered and carried a sense of shame as she said, 'My content isn't the same. It's all surface stuff. Fashion and beauty and travel and all that. My audience isn't the deep, intellectual type, because my content isn't like that anymore …'

Despite herself, Parul felt a small surge of vindication hearing Akki admit that her content had deteriorated in quality since their podcast ended. Parul caught herself, and said feverishly, 'So what! You don't have to be a saint to be believed! You deserve to be believed simply because you're telling the truth.'

'I don't think I can turn their opinion now. Those tapes from Ram and Komal were the last nail on the coffin.'

'No, they weren't! Ram and Komal wouldn't do that on purpose. Have you reached out to them?' Parul's mind was racing. Ram and Komal had liked her more than Akki, because she was a kinder boss, but they didn't hate Akki. They might've thought Akki was a bitch on some days, because, to be fair, she did behave like one sometimes. But Parul was still on good terms with both of them. Ram sometimes helped her with copy-editing. Parul hadn't talked to Komal in a while, but knew how to reach her. She was sure she could get Ram and Komal to clear the air, by providing context to the leaked phone calls.

'No ... I have just been lying low,' Akki said, sounding defeated.

'I'll call them. They probably didn't even say those words with malice. I don't doubt for a second that they'll support us.'

'Us?' The hope in Akki's voice shattered Parul's heart to pieces.

'Us,' Parul said firmly, even as her voice broke. 'We're sisters. We can fight as much as we want, and not talk to each other for an hour or two ... or ten years. But we would still be sisters. I would still be there for you. That would never change.'

Akki wept. Parul joined her, but not for long. She had a plan to make, a rapist to take down. He had abused her sister for years and years, kept her locked, in fear, away from everyone she loved. He couldn't get away with this. Not if Parul had anything to do with it. A plan formed in her head, thoughts scurrying together to build a concrete, sure-fire idea. Dev used to joke about how much of a rule-follower Parul was. A by-the-book, organized loser who could never just wing it and take a risk. Now, Parul planned to employ those same organizational skills and use them against him.

Her body trembled, but she spoke with conviction. 'We'll reunite for a podcast. A new episode. We'll have you, me, Ram and Komal on it, countering every single thing that asshole has said about you, one by one. We'll make an exhaustive list, and we'll go over absolutely everything. Thorough and honest. We'll also shoot a video of the podcast recording, and upload it to YouTube. No time limit. We'll keep the mics and the cameras running for as long as it takes to get all the information out. We will prove him wrong. We also have hours and hours of footage of him on set, exhibiting his manipulative behaviour. I'll watch every single minute till I find something we can use to show the world who he really is. They want an exposé? We'll give them an exposé. And after all this is done, we'll give a copy of the podcast to the police. I'm sorry I wasn't there to help you then. But I'm here now. And I'm not going anywhere.'

The Watering Can

I am out of the danger zone now, but my heart continues to thump loudly in my ears. As soon as the Bhaiya from the shop handed me the ice-cream cone, I turned around and walked away as fast as I could. It usually takes me five minutes to walk home from that shop, but this time, I did it in two minutes, or probably even less than that. I can be really fast when I want to.

When I reach my house, I pull open the main gate – a heavy, black metal one that always gets stuck and you have to pull with all your strength to get it to open. Popo can't open it. He's only three years old, and very small and weak. I'm almost nine, a big brother and a strong boy. I'm the tallest in my class and the strongest, probably. I always win at arm wrestling.

Not as strong as Iron Man yet, but I'm learning. Nishu Bhaiya takes me to watch all the *Avengers* movies, and I take notes in my mind every time. Superheroes are not that different from us. Think about Spider-Man; he's just a school kid who gets bit by a spider and gets his superpowers. And Ant-Man is just a little tiny ant. I'm much bigger than him, so I'm already ahead.

Grown-ups always lecture me that superheroes are not real, and they only exist in comic books and movies. Whenever they tell me that, I agree with them. You have to manage grown-ups, or else they'll never shut up about things. Deep down, I know that superheroes are real. I will be one soon. I just need to grow up and get stronger.

Also, I have to look out for my powers. Powers can come in all kinds of different ways, so I have to stay alert. Nishu Bhaiya says he wants to watch all the *Avengers* movies again. I will watch them with him and find out how every single superhero got their power, because no matter how hard I try, I can't remember how Captain Marvel or Star Lord got their powers. So, this time, I will pay attention and write down as much as I can.

In the stairwell, I rip open the ice-cream cone as I run up to the first floor. I take a bite from the top of the cone. It's just pistachios, almonds and tiny pieces of all kinds of nuts that you have to get through to get to the good part: the ice cream. Bua says dry fruits are good for your brain. I have to eat seven almonds every morning that she soaks in water for me the night before. I don't like it, but arguing with grown-ups gets me nowhere in this family, so I eat the seven almonds every morning and gulp down an entire glass of milk to get rid of the taste. I like milk.

As I enter the house, I finish the dry-fruit parts on the top and finally lick the ice cream. It melts in my mouth and tastes like really cold milk. I close the door behind me and plop on my bed to finish my ice cream. I like the bottom part of the cone with the chocolate.

Before I reach it, the doorbell rings. I am alert. The hairs on the back of my neck stand up from my Spidey sense. I am not out of the danger zone yet. The doorbell rings again. Nishu Bhaiya yells out 'Coming!' to whoever is on the other side of the door.

Where should I hide my ice cream? The cone can't stand up on its own. If I lay it down on the bed or the table, it will melt and spread everywhere. I can't eat it that fast because it's so cold it will make my head freeze. I find a pencil stand on the table and shove the cone upright into it. I run to the mirror and wipe my mouth on the back of my hand. Then, I run to the front door before Nishu Bhaiya gets there.

'Don't open it!' I whisper loudly to Nishu Bhaiya, as he reaches for the door handle.

'Who is it?' Nishu Bhaiya is looking at me. I can't see his eyes clearly, because they are under the shadow of his cap. How angry will he be? Should I tell him now? The doorbell rings again.

The Bhaiya from the shop shouts from the other side. 'Tutu, open the door. I know you're in there. I can see your shadow under the door!'

'Nishu Bhaiya, just give him fifty rupees. I'll explain everything later,' I plead desperately.

'Fifty rupees? What for?' Nishu Bhaiya looks confused.

'I'll tell you later!' I grab his hand to stop him from opening the door.

'Tutu, what did you do?' Now he doesn't look confused. He looks angry. He takes his hand back and opens the door.

I hide behind Nishu Bhaiya. I think about running away to my room and locking the door, finishing my ice cream … but I can't, because they'll make me come out, and yell at me even louder and for longer.

'Nishu ji, Tutu just bought ice cream from my shop with this,' the Bhaiya from the shop says. He's so loud that Baba and Aaji have heard him too. They are coming to the door to see what this is all about – Baba from his study and Aaji from the dining room. I want to turn into a teeny-tiny ant now. Sadly, I don't have my powers yet; I checked this morning by trying to lift the bed.

Nishu Bhaiya is looking at the note the Bhaiya from the shop is holding out. Game over.

'Tutu,' Nishu Bhaiya says. He pulls me from behind him and makes me stand directly in front of the Bhaiya from the shop. I look down at my slippers. I notice how dirty my toenails are as Nishu Bhaiya asks, 'First, you buy ice cream from a shop using fake Monopoly money; then, on top of that, you were trying to bribe Kabir with fifty rupees when you got caught?'

'I thought it was real money. It looks so real,' I mutter weakly in my defence. No one's buying it. I don't know how, but grown-ups somehow always *know*. Even though what I said is believable. The notes from my old games are fake-looking children's notes. But this ₹10 note is from a new game, and looks just like the real one.

'*And* you're lying!' Nishu Bhaiya thunders in a way that makes me stand up straighter. 'That's three things you've done wrong within five minutes!'

Unable to speak, I stand frozen between Nishu Bhaiya and Kabir Bhaiya.

'*Koi baat nahi*,' Kabir Bhaiya says, after already having done all the damage. 'He's just a kid. Must've only been doing *mazaak*.'

'Sorry, Bhaiya,' I say to both Bhaiyas before anyone tells me to. That might give me some brownie points. Grown-ups love it when kids say sorry, and tend to get really angry when we don't say it or say it only after being asked. I have learned from experience that it's best to say sorry as soon as possible every time you get in trouble.

Nishu Bhaiya gives him a real ten-rupee note from his pocket and Kabir Bhaiya leaves, but not before messing up my hair, calling me 'Shaitan!' and laughing like my pain was a joke.

'*Kya hua?*' Aaji asks Nishu Bhaiya.

Once the door closes, I get a loud and long yelling. I feel bad for my mistake, but the note looked so real that I had to try. Bua always says it's good to be curious. I did an experiment and it failed. It's okay to fail, as long as you try. I keep my mouth shut the whole time Nishu Bhaiya yells at me. He calls what I did 'true corrupt politician behaviour' which I don't understand, but don't ask about, because it doesn't sound good.

The rest of the day, I do all kinds of things around the house without being asked. I have to be extra good so that everyone will forgive me and forget what I did. I fill up the watering can in the kitchen sink and carefully carry it, using both my hands, to water the plants in the balcony attached to Nishu Bhaiya's room.

'Tutu, don't walk there!' Aaji says all of a sudden, shocking me into spilling water all over the floor. 'Lily Didi just did *pochha* there. Now you've left footprints all over the floor.'

'And spilled water too!' Lily Didi chimes in. People love to pile on when I'm already getting yelled at. Lily Didi comes every morning and evening to sweep and mop the floors in our house. Usually, she doesn't speak much, but she's chosen this moment to join the attack against me.

'I'll clean it!' I offer.

'Just go. I'll mop it.' Before I can say anything else, she's already walking over to me with the mop in her hand.

'Thank you,' I say, before making my way to the balcony. I start with watering the marigold plant. I'm making swirling movements so that all of the soil in the pot gets the exact same amount of water. Five swirls one way, and then five the other way. I stop before the water overflows and move on to the rose bush. When I get to the tulsi plant, Aaji speaks from behind me. My hands shake again, but I don't spill any water this time. She walks without making any sound. I can never hear her coming. Ever since the lady who does Aaji's massage started coming here, Aaji has stopped wearing her bangles and *payal*. She says they get in the way, and it's a hassle to take them off and put them on again every day. I need to adjust to this change and keep an ear out for the sound of her slippers.

'I just watered them this morning,' she says.

'But they needed more water. They were dying,' I say.

'If you give them too much water, the roots will rot. Tutu … I'm saying something. Stop watering them!'

'Aaji, please. I know what I'm doing. I'm old enough,' I say. I move on to a plant with just leaves and no flowers. I don't know its name, but it could be a snake plant or a money plant. Or maybe a spider plant. I've heard those names from Bua.

'Tutu, listen to your Aaji,' Nishu Bhaiya jumps in. See? Everybody just wants to yell at me. I was born to get yelled at. Maybe that's my superpower. A completely useless one. 'Do you think *you* know more about plants or Aaji?'

'I know about *these* plants,' I challenge him, pointing to the plants I've just watered. I won't let getting-yelled-at become my superpower. Every superhero needs to stand up and defend themselves. What kind of superhero gets yelled at and stays quiet? No superhero. Just a regular boy. 'I can take care of these plants. I do it every day.'

'Really? I've only seen you water them one or two times in … your whole life.'

This might be true, but I don't back down. 'Okay, let's do a competition. You give me two plants to keep in my room, and if I keep them safe and perfect for one month, you'll … you'll give me one thing.'

'What thing?' Nishu Bhaiya tilts his head to the side. He's acting all serious, but I know he's smiling inside. He's always pulling my leg. That's what Bua always says when I complain to her about him; that he's only joking around and pulling my leg because I get bothered by it. So, I don't get bothered by it anymore. Or at least I pretend not to.

'Any one thing? I haven't decided yet. It can be a nerf gun or a bat or a video game or nachos or a bobblehead or anything,' I say all the ideas my brain is coming up with out loud.

'Okay, deal.'

'Deal,' I say in my adult voice, and shake Nishu Bhaiya's hand.

'Which plants do you want to adopt?'

'Any two plants.'

'Okay, then.'

Nishu Bhaiya chooses two plants – both just leaves and no flowers – and carries them to my bedroom. He puts them on the windowsill next to my bed. I'm being overconfident, but my teacher says that plants only need three important things: water, air and sunlight. These plants already have air and sunlight. All they need is water. I will water them every morning before going to school, and, in one month, I will win the competition.

All I have to worry about is deciding what I will make Nishu Bhaiya buy for me when he loses. My head is swirling with ideas. I could get that airplane Lego set my friend has, or a Captain America hoodie, or anything else I want. I will make a list to help me pick. Otherwise, I will never be able to fall asleep at night.

🌹

This is easy. I wake up every morning all on my own when my alarm rings, even before Papa has to come to wake me up. I keep the watering can right under the window. I have only had to fill it up once and it has lasted me four days. Both plants look green and happy. I pull the curtains back, so that they will get sunlight when the sun comes out while I'm in school.

Today, my watering can is full; I filled it last night because I'm taking this seriously. I pour the same amount of water into both plant pots and put the watering can back under the window. I have to do this only twenty-five more times and get whatever I want from Nishu Bhaiya. As superhero tasks go, mine is pretty easy.

❀

'Popo, no!'

'Yes, *I* want to water the plant!' Popo says in his sugar-sweet whiny voice that works on everyone else, but not on me. I know that voice. It's the voice I used to use on grown-ups, but not anymore. Ever since Popo was born, if I try to talk like that to plead for something, everyone gets annoyed and says, 'Are you a little baby?'

'No, Popo! It's not a toy,' I say in the stern voice Papa uses on me. I pick up Popo's Hot Wheels car and put it in his little hand. 'Play with this.'

As soon as I take the watering can from him, he starts crying. I know it's not a real cry; it's the type of cry that gets me in trouble. He only stops after he gets his way. Not this time.

'What's going on?' Papa asks from the door a minute later. He looks from me to Popo, then back at me. 'What did you do?'

'I didn't do anything. Popo is being *ziddi*. He's trying to pick up the watering can, but it's heavy and I need it to water my plants. It's a big-boy job, not for little Popo.' I say everything really fast so that Papa will have to listen before he yells at me for making Popo cry.

'Popo, stop crying,' Papa says. I can tell that he's busy and needs to get back to work. He's already turning around when he says, 'Play with your Hot Wheels and don't bother Tutu Bhaiya.'

Popo continues to cry for a little longer, but without any real interest. Everyone says that he looks exactly like me when I was his age. Some people also say that even now we look exactly the same, but I don't see it. The only thing we have exactly the same is our hairstyle, and that's only because Papa takes us to the barber who sits outside under the peepal tree and gives us both ugly, round katori-cuts.

I pick up the watering can and peek into the pots. One of the plants has shed four leaves. I look at that plant closely and notice that some of its other leaves are turning yellow at the tips. Not as yellow as the leaves that have fallen into the pot, but not as green as the other plant's leaves.

I pour extra water in that plant, pick up the fallen leaves and throw them away in the trash can in the kitchen. I have accidentally skipped watering my plants one or two times, ever since I started going to cricket classes after school. It's two hours long, from 3 p.m. to 5 p.m., and I get really tired from it, which means I need more sleep at night. Then, I wake up late in the morning, and have to run around and get ready, eat breakfast and pack my bag really fast. I forget to water my plants before leaving for school. After school, it's the same thing all over again: I have to go to cricket practice, take a bath, do my homework, watch TV, eat dinner and go to sleep. My life has become much busier than it was when the competition first began. But I can't let anymore leaves fall. I have to get back on track and win this.

🌹

More leaves are falling. I keep watering the plant every morning. I sit next to it and sing to it, just like my friend told me he saw on TV. It doesn't help. I don't want to ask Aaji or Nishu Bhaiya, because they will probably just tell me that I'm losing the competition because I'm not old enough to take care of plants on my own.

Instead, I sneak up to the terrace to watch Baba garden. I watch the way he takes care of all the hundreds of different plants he's grown. He grows flowers, brinjals, green chillies, tomatoes and ladyfingers. He also grows strawberries, but they look smaller than the ones in my books, and taste sour, but we tell Baba that they are sweet and delicious to make him smile.

I try to write down how much water he gives to every plant, but it's all different and I can't keep track. Some plants, he waters every day. Others, every other day, or even once a week. He moves some of the pots around. He digs the soil of some plants and mixes more smelly soil from a bag into it. He has all these grown-up tools to take care of his garden. He calls them *belacha* and *khurapi* and weird names like that. I don't have any of that for my plants and, even if I did, I wouldn't know what to do with them. Won't digging the soil make the roots come out and die? It's too hard to learn how to do all of these different things.

In the end, I come back downstairs, pick up all the newly fallen leaves and throw them in the trash can. Seventeen, I counted. Then, I look at the dying plant carefully. There are fourteen leaves that look like they're about to fall down. I find Fevicol from Papa's cupboard and stick the fourteen at-risk leaves to their twigs.

❀

I'm playing Jenga with Popo. We're not playing the way the rules on the little piece of paper that came in the box tell us, because Popo is too small to play games properly. We've made our own game with our own rules using the Jenga blocks. This is how it goes: we divide the Jenga blocks between the two of us. I build a wall or a house or a castle with my blocks and once I'm finished building, Popo throws his blocks at them to break down whatever I've built.

It's really fun. Every time he hits my structure, and everything comes falling down, Popo laughs loudly and rolls around on the floor. I'm having fun too.

The plants on the windowsill are looking at me. I don't look back. The competition ends in eight days and my plant only has six leaves left. I counted this morning. It's all sticks now. There are no green leaves left. The soil is soaked in water, bright sunlight is pouring in through the window and there's plenty of air in the room, from the fan I have turned on, but the plant is still dying. I can't think of anything else I can do. Nothing works.

Popo is really quiet today. He is usually never this quiet. I look at him to check if he's okay. Sometimes, when he's really quiet, it means he's doing something bad, like putting something in his mouth or breaking something.

Popo is looking at me.

'*Kya hua*?' I ask him. My voice comes out weird and broken.

'No,' Popo says. He reaches out to touch my face. He rubs the tears on my cheek and shakes his head.

I don't want to cry, but I can't stop. This is so silly. My little brother doesn't need to make me stop crying. That's not how this works. My plants are dying, I have to throw away my list of wishes, Nishu Bhaiya will call me a loser and everyone will say that I'm not big enough to do anything. I cry more, but then Popo jumps on me. He covers my eyes and mouth with his small hands to make me stop crying. I fall backwards on the floor, holding my little brother tightly in my arms, and we roll around in fits of laughter.

🌹

On the last day of the competition, I knock on Nishu Bhaiya's door. My plan is simple. I will tell him what has happened despite my best efforts. I will accept that I lost and watch him laugh at me. I tried my best, and that's all I can ever do, like Bua always tells me.

When Nishu Bhaiya doesn't answer, I push the door open. His room is empty. He's not here. Now I have to wait to tell him. I walk over to his gaming chair and climb up on it. I push away from the table using my hands and spin in the chair as fast as I can. Soon, I feel dizzy. My feet don't reach the floor, so I can't use them to stop. And I've spun too far away from the table, so my hands can't reach anything either.

'Need help?' Baba calls from the door.

'Yes, please!' I call back from the spinning chair.

He rescues me by stopping the chair. I climb out and collapse on the bed to make my head stop spinning. Baba sits down on Nishu Bhaiya's chair. I have never seen him do that before. He usually only sits in his own chair in his study. At the dining table, he sits at the same chair for every meal. He sleeps in his own bed for his afternoon nap and at nights. I sit up on the bed and pay attention.

'What are you doing?' I ask.

'I've seen you lurk around the terrace when I'm gardening. Is there something you want from me?' Baba asks in his calm voice. Even though he's not smiling, his voice sounds like he's smiling.

'Not anymore,' I say flatly. 'I've already lost the competition. My plant's dead now.' As I say this, my voice shakes. I clear my throat to push it away. Nobody likes it when I cry;

everyone always tells me to stop, but sometimes I can't stop. Like right now, no matter how hard I try, tears collect in my eyes and flow down my cheeks. I wipe them away angrily, but then my lips begin to shake. This is impossible to stop.

'Your plant?' Baba asks, but I'm crying too hard now to answer. I've been crying alone in my room, and when I do that, it's easy for me to stop after one minute, but now that Baba is here, watching me, I can't stop. He gets up from the chair and sits on the bed next to where I'm lying. 'What happened? Why are you crying?' he asks. All I can think about is that I've never seen him sit on this bed before.

'Tutu, what's wrong?' Baba asks.

It takes me a second, but I sit up, wipe my cheeks and sniff the boogers back into my nose. Then, I tell Baba everything. How nobody believes that I'm special. How they tell me I'm too small to do anything. I tell him about the competition, the plants, the watering can and falling leaves. I tell him everything.

Baba listens to everything, but doesn't speak when I stop speaking. He thinks for a minute, then says, 'Not every plant needs the same things to thrive.'

I don't know what thrive means, but I understand what he's saying from the first part of his sentence. 'What did my plant need?' I ask.

'I don't know, I don't know what kind of plant it is. I'll take a look if you want me to. There still might be a way to save it. Most plants are resilient, with strong roots. Even if they look like they're dead, they can have life inside them.'

'Really? Even the plants without any leaves? Just stems?'

'It's possible. We can take a look.'

Wow. I feel better already. I've lost the competition, but there's still a chance I can save my plant and prove everyone wrong. 'Yes, I want to know what happened. I want to fix it!' I jump off the bed. 'Let's go! I watered the plant every day. Sometimes, I watered it two or even three times a day, but the leaves kept falling. Do you think it needed more water? The other plant stayed green with only a little bit of water.'

'Too much water can also cause the roots to decay,' Baba says.

I turn around. He hasn't got up to go look at the plant. 'What does decay mean?' I ask.

Baba looks at me. Then he says, 'Nothing, it's not important. It's most likely not what happened to your plant.' I relax, and Baba pats the space next to him on the bed. I walk back to him and sit down at the spot he patted. 'There's a lesson to be learned here. Do you know what it is?'

I shake my head.

'It's that we're all different, even plants. We all need different things to sustain us, make us happy. Your two plants are a great example to demonstrate this. Both of them received the same things, more or less. You cared for both of them. Yet, one of them flourished, and the other perished. One is doing great, while the other isn't. This shows us that we all need different things.'

I nod thoughtfully. I don't like it when Baba uses grown-up words, but he always explains it in normal words too, so I can understand. He's talking about plants, but he keeps saying *us*. Just like in Moral Studies period, we read stories about animals, but, in the end, the teaches always compares it to us, people.

'What do we need?' I ask.

'You tell me? What do you think you need?'

I think about it. I need to come up with an intelligent answer to impress Baba. He's very smart – a professor with a 'Dr' in front of his name – not at all easily impressed. What do I need? I can't think of anything. I make myself think harder, and finally find something I *don't* need. 'I don't think I need … cricket classes,' I say slowly, watching Baba's face.

Baba chuckles, and I relax. He asks, 'Why do you say that?'

'Because I get tired! It's so hot outside, and the field is dirty and dusty. It gets in my eyes and nose and hair and clothes and shoes. The older Bhaiyas don't let us younger players play. They do batting and bowling, and make us do fielding all the time. Sometimes, they let me bat, but then they throw the ball really fast, or spin it all wonky. Then they laugh if I can't make a run. When I come home, Papa complains about how dirty my uniform is, and Aaji says I'm getting darker and darker in the sun every day. I fall asleep while doing homework, and one time I even fell asleep in class when I was really tired, and the teacher gave me punishment for it. She made me stand outside for the rest of the period.' I didn't know I was going to say all this, but the words just come out and I can't stop them.

'Sounds like you've made up your mind.' Baba sounds impressed. It makes me feel smart and grown-up. 'What are you going to do about it?'

'I'll tell Papa!' I say confidently. 'Will he be mad? Will you come with me?'

'I will come with you if you need me to.' Baba gets up and holds out his hand. I get up too, sliding my hands in his rough, gardening hand.

'Wait! What if Papa asks what I want to do instead of cricket? Everyone has to do *something*. Aashi goes to painting classes, but I get too bored. I used to go to dance classes, but my body hurts too much at night … I have to find something else, or else Papa will never let me quit cricket.'

'Well, I know you're not small anymore. You're a big boy. But there's still plenty of time for us to find out what you need. Don't worry. We'll think about it together.' Baba smiles down at me and squeezes my hand.

We have to tell Papa about cricket. He will be mad, because he already bought me all the gear. The uniform, bat, helmet, shoes and pads. But I will be honest with him and tell him that I only like playing with my friends, kids my age. When I play with the Bhaiyas, I don't have any fun and get double tired. Bua says we don't have to be very good at our hobbies; we can just have fun. I will tell Papa that. And with Baba by my side, I know Papa won't yell at me that much. As we go to find Papa, I start making a list of things that I might want to do instead of cricket. It has to be something cool, and something that will help me prepare for the time when I finally get my superpowers.

Made for Each Other

'What's the scene like out there?' Avani asked, looking up as Shraddha walked into the room and sat down on the carpet next to her.

'Everyone's having fun. The DJ is playing old SRK songs. In fact, some people are having *too much fun*, if you know what I mean.'

'I don't. What do you mean?'

'I saw Teeni pour whisky or some such spirit in a half-empty two-litre Coca-Cola bottle. They've been passing it around. Some of them are definitely super wasted.'

'Oh God, are you serious? I told Ravi to make sure his friends behaved themselves. Honestly, they act so *gawar*, rowdy, wherever they go. I told Ravi so clearly, so many times, not to let them do that here.'

'It's not … that bad, to be fair. They're just dancing.'

'For now! It'll only escalate. You don't know them, Shraddha. You can't take them anywhere. I knew we shouldn't have invited them here to our family home, with everyone here.'

'They're here now though, so just don't think about it.'

'How can I not! They'll make fools of themselves and us, in front of everyone. They'll only get rowdier the more they drink—'

'Okay, okay, relax, Avani *di*! I'll go find Ravi *Jiju* and tell him to control his friends.' Shraddha got up and left promptly. When she returned a few minutes later, Avani was still breathing hard. Shraddha asked tentatively, 'Is anything else bothering you? Are you nervous about getting married or something?'

'No, I'm not nervous about getting married or something!' Avani snapped at her younger cousin. 'We're already married! We've been married for two years!'

Shraddha stared wide-eyed at Avani, and then at the two other people in the room, the girls applying mehndi on each of Avani's palms. They didn't look up, probably accustomed to being treated as invisible beings.

'*Kisi ko kuch bolna mat.* I'll tip you extra for keeping your mouth shut,' Avani said to them shortly before turning back to Shraddha. 'What? Are you just going to stand there? Don't you want to know what happened?'

'Are you going to keep yelling at me or will you calm down?'

Avani smiled despite herself. This is why she liked Shraddha the most in their family. Shraddha was twenty-five, and didn't care that she was five years younger than Avani; she wasn't a pushover. Even though she would have been dying to find out more details about this juicy new revelation, she focused on her self-respect first.

'Come sit,' Avani said, nodding towards a spot next to her.

Shraddha lowered herself to the floor again. 'Don't make me get up again for a while. The baby's kicking like crazy.'

Avani's eyes darted to Shraddha's belly. She wished she could rub it, but the fresh mehndi made it impossible. 'Don't you want to know? This has been my big secret for two years.'

'You've been married for two years? How is that possible? Tell me everything.'

'Everything … will take a long time.' Avani looked at her hands. She was going to be immobile for at least two more hours. She really shouldn't be talking about this in front of strangers, and yet, she couldn't hold it in any longer. Besides, the mehndi girls would probably not even understand most of what they were saying in English. Avani didn't have the energy to care anymore. She was exhausted to the bone. 'Well, there was this whole thing with this other girl …'

'Jiju cheated on you?' Shraddha whispered sharply.

'Shh! And yes, not only cheat, like, once or twice by mistake. He had a full-fledged affair with this other girl he used to work with. Actually, technically, I was the other woman. When I found out, they had been together for two and a half years. And we had been together for two years. So she came first. She was cheated on; I was cheated with.'

Shraddha was stunned into silence.

'And, oh, you'll love this – the way I found out was hilarious. I mean if it weren't so tragic, it would've been hilarious. So, get this – I never trusted him in the beginning, right? He's reasonably good-looking, not in a traditional way, but he has money and is successful. He wouldn't be so cute without those things, right? So, when we first met,

I was twenty-seven and he was twenty-six. Still young and dumb about relationships. He seemed like a player from the beginning. Super flirtatious, too focused on sex. And I, in my situation, thought that if I gave him whatever he wanted now, I could eventually get him to become serious about us. I wasn't really going to waste too much time on someone who just wanted to dick around and have fun.'

Shraddha didn't interrupt.

Avani continued, 'So I did the whole thing with him. Clubbing, crazy sex stuff; he was obsessed with blow jobs, so I had my work cut out for me.'

Shraddha's eyes widened to a point where they were at risk of popping out of their sockets.

'I'll spare you the details, but it was … a significant amount of work. But, like, I wasn't exactly easy either. You've gotta have mystery; so I gave him the hot and cold treatment. I was pretty high maintenance, and he had had to earn everything he got, you know? Anyway, after all of that, we finally fell into a rhythm. Maybe six to eight months after we first hooked up, we finally became official. Like, exclusive. Met each other's friends and everything. Still kept everything off social media though at his insistence, because we didn't want our parents to find out. I didn't find such behaviour suspicious, because many people I knew would do the same. I wasn't exactly dying for my parents in Jalandhar to find out about my boyfriend in Delhi.'

'And all this time, he already had a girlfriend?'

'Yep. That wasn't really real though; it was long distance. They met maybe once every six months, but apparently, they talked on the phone a lot. Like, several times a day, so she was fully invested. I knew of her existence. Really pretty girl, who once worked with Ravi – I followed her on Facebook. But it wasn't until much later that I asked her for her number. I called her and asked point-blank if there was something between them. And she denied it. She said nope, he's all yours.'

'But didn't you say …?'

'Yeah, there's more drama to the story. Fast-forward to two months later, she calls me out of the blue. I don't answer, because Ravi had told me that she was a little crazy and was obsessed with him. So, I blocked her on WhatsApp. But then, she messaged me on Facebook, and spilled the beans. Well, actually, all she said in the message was that she had lied to me when I called her earlier, and she felt guilty about that, so she just wanted to tell me the truth, that yes, something had been going on between them. They had been together for two and a half years, and that they had broken up just a month before I called her. And so, I called Ravi, and added her to the conference call. Everything came out then.'

Avani paused to release a long breath and the words she had held close to her chest for two years came pouring out of her. 'Apparently, she knew of me as his friend's girlfriend. So, she never questioned my presence in his life. Also, she was, like, twenty-two at the time – this is two years ago. Ravi was twenty-eight, and I was twenty-nine. This girl just sounded like this naive, idealistic kid, who got caught in his web of lies and had her heart broken. He had told her that I was crazy and suicidal, that I had tried to drink phenyl on three different occasions, and so she stayed away from me. And he'd told me that she was crazy and obsessed with him, so I stayed away from her … for the most part. But I ended up calling her when I had this nagging gut feeling I couldn't shake off, and she called me two months later with the truth. That was all it took for this mess to blow up in my face. That two-hour-long conference call was brutal.'

'How did you go from that to marrying him?' Shraddha asked in disbelief, clutching her belly, as if seeking support from her unborn child.

'Okay, don't judge me!'

'I'm not judging! I'm just trying to understand.'

'Listen, I weighed my options, okay? Love and all is good, but reality is a bitch. I was twenty-nine, and had already wasted two years on this guy. Throughout that conference call, he consistently maintained that he loved me, and she was just exaggerating and being crazy. Like, of course, I didn't believe most of what he was saying, but, at the end of the day, he chose me and made her look crazy. It could've been the other way round as well. But, like, I didn't want him to have the power, now that I finally had a clear upper hand in our relationship – so I broke up with him. And that made him chase me. He would call me all the time, send me gifts and flowers and texts. I had so much power, and I loved being on my high horse, to be honest. I kept in touch with her too, to make sure she was fine. She was the one who had broken up with him, right? Even before I had called her, he was ignoring her too much and treating her badly. So all of the new information she was provided with about his cheating only helped her realize that she had made the right decision and moving on was easier. She and I texted all through the day. She was young, was applying to go abroad for a master's degree. But I ... I didn't have many options. I don't have a college degree and being a flight attendant wasn't going to be a permanent career ... Our profession has a shelf life. Airline companies in India are obsessed with hot, young air hostesses. I weighed my options and based on how much attention he was giving me, and the fact that, hello, I want babies and I wasn't getting any younger, I said I'll take him back only if he committed fully and married me. So, he did.'

'And that was two years ago.'

'Yep. We had to wait for the real wedding because we still needed to figure out where we would live, when we would have kids; our parents needed to meet, I had to plan the wedding – all of that. Meanwhile, we used my flight attendant privileges to take trips to different vacation spots across Europe. It was a pretty sweet deal. He paid for hotels and stuff, I got us free tickets. Sex was still fine. I wasn't as generous, but I didn't need to be, because I had so much power. I feel like I actually had more power these past two years being secretly married to him than I will after this public wedding. Like, now he knows I can't go anywhere.'

'Do you want to?'

'Mmm, I don't know. I don't know what I want.' Avani sighed and checked her hands. The mehndi girls had moved on to the backs of her hands.

'Wow. That's a lot. I ... don't even know what to tell you,' Shraddha said, studying Avani's face. You think you know someone. When her older cousin had left home to become a flight attendant, their family's reaction had been mixed: the older generation looked down on the service industry, the short skirts and the general freedom given to girls, and the younger generation had been in awe, dreaming of their own future escape. Shraddha had never been able to escape. Instead, she was married at the age of twenty-one, had her first child two years later, and was now carrying her second, all before she turned twenty-six. Avani's life had gone in a completely different direction. This glamour of travel, affairs, sex and secret marriages ... Shraddha had only known these to exist in twisted romance novels.

'He said he would change. Back then. He promised. And you know how he is. When he gives you his full attention, there's no escape. He can be so charming.' Avani looked at Shraddha for confirmation.

Shraddha bit her lower lip. To her, he sounded like a scumbag, but she kept that observation to herself. They were already married, so there was no point in saying anything. 'Do you love him?' she finally asked.

'Yes. And he loves me. I'm telling you, he does. Why else would he have gone to such extremes to win me back? Just for free flight tickets?' Avani snorted.

Shraddha smiled back.

Avani said thoughtfully, 'He is pretty cheap. Like he wants to look rich, but if he didn't absolutely need to spend money, he wouldn't. But that's good, right? For our kids.'

Shraddha's heart sank further with every new piece of information Avani offered. 'And you both want kids for sure?'

'Yes! Like, right now. I'm thirty-one and we want both our kids to be born before I turn thirty-five. That way I can get my body back fast. And then I'm free to do whatever I want.'

'What does that mean?'

Avani paused to think of the best way to explain it. 'Look, I'm not stupid. I zoom out and look at my life. Let's say I live till I am seventy … eighty years old. I can only have kids probably for a few more years. But once I have them, I can do other things. I have the rest of my life. Thirty-five … forty years. I've already given him some of the best years of my life; so what's some more? Sure, it'll be great if things with Ravi work out. But if they don't, worst-case scenario: we get divorced after I have our kids. That way, he's tied to me with child support and spouse support and what not. Flight attendants' careers decline after a certain age. And, as I have come to realize, serving drinks to assholes is hardly a dream job anyway. Not to mention cleaning up and being polite and smiling … Ugh, don't even get me started on all the smiling.'

'Wait, I don't follow. What were you saying about divorce?'

'Right, yeah. Worst-case scenario. But it's not so bad, right? Considering we're already legally married, breaking up now means getting a divorce anyway. So why not give it a few more years and then reconsider? Who else am I going to find at such short notice? My biological clock is ticking fast.'

'You're only going through with this wedding for kids?' It was difficult for Shraddha to hide her disdain.

'No, of course not!' Avani exclaimed defensively. 'I do love him. I've always loved him. I was so madly in love with him

when all of this drama first went down. That's why I took
him back, married him. It was so bad when we had broken
up for a couple of months and his phone calls stopped ... I
literally couldn't wake up in the morning and get out of bed.
He was so gentle with me. Like we always had a relationship
of extremes. High highs and low lows.'

Shraddha nodded. Everything Avani said was churning
in her head. She couldn't fully make sense of things. 'And
... where are you now? Thinking about divorce?'

'No, not really. That's just the worst-case scenario I'm
telling myself; just in case, to help myself get over this cold
feet or whatever.' When Shraddha didn't look convinced,
Avani added quickly, 'Listen, I'm fine, really. We're in love.
We're excited to have kids and live together. There's so much
to look forward to. I was just thinking that it was probably
a little more exciting being secretly married. Felt more
dangerous. But this will be fine too. I can take a break while
we have kids and then eventually quit my job. And Ravi said
he wants me to take some distance-learning courses, so that
I can get a bachelor's degree. Oh God, that was a dramatic
fight too. I accused him of being embarrassed of me and he
tried to convince me that he only wanted the best for me, and
to give me the opportunities I might not have had before.
So, he'll pay for my education. And he'll actually also pay to
promote my social media. I could, like, do modelling and ads
and stuff. There are so many things you can do online now.'

Shraddha inhaled deeply. The baby was kicking. Her
life couldn't be more different from Avani's. After this

conversation, Shraddha felt thankful for the normality in her life. Sure, it wasn't nearly as dynamic as her cousin's, but at least her relationship didn't have a trace of infidelity or betrayal either. And, in that moment, it felt like a true blessing. She sighed, rubbing her bump. In any case, she was invested in Avani's story now, and wanted to see how it ended. In order to remain in Avani's good graces, and be privy to her future secrets, she had to hide her judgement and show her support. She said, 'Listen, it sounds like you know what you're doing. Given everything, I agree: it's best to go through with the public wedding ceremony. You can always revaluate the marriage in a few years. You'll actually be in a better position then. Get your education, and your social media following. Plus, with the pregnancies out of the way, there's no ticking clock, and, like you said, he'll have to pay child and spouse support. You can quit your job, and like … date?'

'Yes,' Avani said with conviction. 'But like I said, that's the worst-case scenario. I'd obviously want the marriage to actually work out.'

'Obviously.'

'Because I love him. I just don't trust him. I can't, after everything …' Avani was thinking about the messages she'd found on his phone just the week before. She kept that part to herself.

'You'll be fine. And I'm always here whenever you need to talk,' Shraddha said, dropping her head on Avani's shoulder and inspecting her mehndi. She mulled over everything

she had learned during this interaction. All said and done,
no one was completely innocent in this situation. It really
sounded like Avani and Ravi deserved each other. Shraddha
would even go as far as to say that they were made for
each other.

How Would They Know?

'So, this is it? Your last night of freedom!' Mohit slapped Ravi on his back. His voice was barely audible over the thumping beats of the music. The bass reverberated inside their chests, the air was humid from the steam released through nozzles situated strategically around the nightclub, making the light effects look especially dreamy. Ravi was surrounded by the sweaty, dancing bodies of his friends and cousins.

'Looks like it,' Ravi shrugged dismissively.

'Arey, his life is *toh* full *aish* only!' one of the other boys roared. 'The wife-to-be is full-on hotness, and then there's the matter of the free flight tickets ...'

'The world is literally at your feet, na? How does it feel, Mr World-travelling Overachiever?'

'Pretty good. Not gonna lie!' Ravi said with a smile. But his jaws were clenched, hiding the saltiness he felt. The way his closest, oldest friends and cousins were behaving, loud and obnoxious, was getting under Ravi's skin. He had to keep reminding himself that this would only last another day. Within twenty-four hours, he would be free of his drunk, boisterous companions.

Ravi would be transferred to a different type of prison, tied to a tall (half-an-inch taller than him, a fact he deeply resented) woman who would continue to bear grievances and look at him with dissatisfaction through eyes half-hidden under the thick lashes she stuck to her eyelids with scary-looking blue-coloured glue. He couldn't remember the last time he saw her without those eye umbrellas. Or without a fully painted face. At the moment, she was nowhere in his vicinity, and yet, when he pictured her, Ravi could actually smell her overwhelming designer perfume.

He used to admire her meticulous attention to detail when it came to doing her hair and make-up when they first met. As a flight attendant, she had to follow the exact same make-up routine every time she had to fly, which was every time they saw each other. That's what drew her to him in the first place. Just the memory of her arriving in Delhi, walking towards him in her high heels, her trolley suitcase trailing right behind her aroused Ravi even now. He used to drive her back to his apartment and promptly undress her, mess up her perfectly lined bright-red lipstick, undo her bun and let her long black hair loose. But leave her stockings on. The following day, when it was time for her next flight, she used to sit in front of the mirror in his bedroom for hours putting everything back together. He would watch her every step, imagine reversing everything she was doing, when she would return a few days later.

Avani was undeniably hot. All his male friends thought so, and all their girlfriends were jealous of her. That felt good. That was a gratification Ravi never had growing up as a fat kid. It felt like a dream, redemption. So, Ravi clung to her hotness, focused on it, while ignoring the qualities he had wanted in his dream girl, qualities that Avani didn't possess. Like the kind of traditional Indian, Bollywood kind of beauty he wanted. The plane of her face was ... flat. He had never noticed the plane of anyone's face before, didn't think it mattered, until Avani had become a permanent part of his life. He tried his best not to compare it to a horse's. It was difficult, as his brain conjured up side-by-side images of Avani's face and the face of a large brown horse. The horse-like shape wasn't the only thing he had had to get used to. There were a few other little quirks: her eyes were small and close together, her nose was giant and when she smiled, the gums in her upper jaw showed quite unattractively.

Ravi shook his head. He couldn't be focusing too much on these thoughts the night before their wedding. Avani knew she wasn't exactly beautiful, so she put in a lot of work to look hot instead. Tight clothes, long hair, lean frame, designer brands – she did it all to compensate. And it worked. He wasn't exactly Hrithik Roshan either. Who was he to nitpick?

Besides, she knew her best angles, and used the right photo-editing apps, so in still photos, she looked downright smoking. That's what really mattered. Only a few people see you in real life. Hundreds and thousands and millions of people can see you online. If she kept at it, she could be a big influencer one day. Money, fame, free products – they could have it all.

Ravi had been vigilant about his alcohol intake that night. Avani would kill him if he had a hangover on their wedding day. So, he had rationed his drinking and sipped slowly on one drink every forty-five minutes. Six straight hours of drinking later, as he found himself holding his ninth glass of whisky, he tried to remember why he had agreed to this. The two main reasons he was going through with the wedding were (1) to maintain his superior position in his friends' group, and (2) they were already married, so the wedding was only sealing the deal for society. He had no control over what was happening or how to stop it. If he was honest with himself, as much as he hated this, he didn't, in fact, want to stop it. With her many, many flaws, Avani did love him in a manic, obsessive kind of way. And Ravi was the type of person who needed to be loved in a manic, obsessive kind of way. It nourished him, fed his ego. Overall, it was an okay deal for him.

'Pakka, you don't want to come?' Mohit leaned forward and screamed in Ravi's direction. His thick black beard was wet with spilled beer, the whites of his eyes were now more red than their original colour. None of that was enough to get him to pause. He continued unabashedly, 'The *setting* is not bad. You should join us!'

'No, thank you. You all go ahead. Have fun with the *setting*.' Ravi checked the time on his phone: 2.17 a.m. Time for him to return to his suite and pass out. One last night of having the whole bed to himself, before he had to go to sleep with the same person every night, for the rest of their lives.

'Come on, yaar! None of your *saaliyans* are anywhere in sight. No one will tell Bhabhi ji what you are up to tonight!'

'That's right. And, like I said, the setting is not bad at all. These girls are all foreigners.' Mohit winked at him.

Ravi looked around at his group of friends and cousins. Not one of them was in his senses. Even if he hadn't been worried about getting caught, Ravi wouldn't want to spend time with these obliterated idiots. This night was a disaster waiting to happen and he had the good sense to check out of that narrative.

'No, thank you,' he said firmly. He didn't bother to smile. They were too wasted to get their feelings hurt by his rudeness anyway. 'You all go ahead.'

His circle of assorted friends and cousins retreated from around him, palms up in surrender. They muttered, loudly enough for Ravi to hear over the music in the underground nightclub, things like 'your loss' and 'whatever, man' before they left.

Ravi turned to his drink. It was fresh. The single ice cube at the bottom of the glass hadn't even begun melting yet. He swirled it around and watched the edges of the cube hit the inside of the glass. He was mesmerized. He watched the cube dancing in the glass for a long time, longer than a man in his senses would care to. Maybe he should skip this drink and go to bed instead; he clearly didn't need it.

Ravi set the glass down determinedly and looked up. His head swam from the sudden motion. He definitely didn't need this drink. As he made to get up from the bar stool, his eyes caught sight of a cloud of pink across the bar. It was hair. Big, curly, a mountain of hair, perched on top of a fairy-like face. Was she an actual fairy? Her lips were full and shiny, alight in the glow of the candle that sat in front of her. Her eyes were big, her lashes were a normal length, not dwarfing her eyes. He made a note to tell Avani that her extra-premium long lashes made her eyes look smaller. He wanted to take a photo of this girl to show Avani for reference. But was this girl real? Would she even show up in a photograph?

But then again, even if he did manage to take a photo and show it to Avani, it's not like Avani would suddenly learn how to take constructive criticism. She would just get really *really* angry all of a sudden, going from a zero to a hundred, and once she was done being furious with him, she would dive deep into the emotional melodrama phase. She would sob, call him toxic, and tell him he didn't love her and accept her the way she was, even after everything she does for him. In turn, he would get defensive and tell her that he never asked her to do any of the excessive things she does, and she only did those things for herself to begin with. Then they would just go around in circles, arguing about everything the other had ever done wrong in their lives. That is how it always went. It was not worth it.

Ravi checked the time again. It was best for him to call it a day. And yet, he couldn't bring himself to get up and leave. He didn't want the night to end. Because when the night ended, it would be his wedding day.

Ravi slid off his stool and looked up. The fairy was gone. Figured. She had probably just been a figment of his imagination anyway.

'Want some company?' a sweet, clear voice said next to him. Ravi spun towards it. It was the fairy. He was surprised to find that such a small body could produce such a commanding voice. He would have to shout to be heard in this loud club.

Ravi found himself incapable of producing a response, other than the strange croak that escaped his throat.

The fairy smiled encouragingly. Her green eyes looked at him patiently.

Green eyes. Ravi had never met someone with green eyes before. The only person he had known to have green eyes was Harry Potter. Ravi shook his head to get rid of the image of round, metal-framed spectacles his brain was conjuring.

Ravi cleared his throat. 'Sure,' he said, sounding very unsure. 'I can have another drink.'

'Oh, I meant company in your room tonight, but a drink before we do that is a great idea.' With that, the fairy leaned over the bar and grabbed two shot glasses. She walked over, in her high heels, hips swinging, to the liquor taps across the bar and filled both glasses with clear liquids.

Ravi looked around to check if someone was watching them steal drinks. He was staying at this resort, along with all their wedding guests. After the fairy disappeared into the night, he would be the one facing the repercussions of thievery. He wondered what Avani would have to say about petty theft.

'Is this tequila?' he asked meekly when she returned.

She held out a glass to him, raised hers and said, 'Salut!'

Before Ravi had a chance to respond, she inverted her glass into her open mouth and gulped. Ravi watched with fascination, the movement of her exposed throat as she swallowed. He followed suit, not wanting to look uncool in front of the coolest person he'd ever met.

'Ready?' Big green eyes looked up at him.

'For …?' he murmured. His brain, under the influence of alcohol, was processing information with much difficulty. Did this fairy really want to go to his room with him? Who was she? Where had she come from? Why was she so interested in him?

'Some company. Some fun. You're staying in this hotel, no?' Her voice was raspy, light like air.

'Yes, but … I'm …' Ravi gulped. His mouth was dry. The back of his throat burned with the tequila. He wasn't a fan of clear liquor. Gathering all of his restrain, he declared, 'I'm taken.'

'How cute!' The fairy burst into laughter that looked and sounded musical, out of this world. Even though she was laughing at him, it didn't feel offensive. On the contrary, it convinced him that he was being silly. 'I'm hardly asking you to marry me! Are you going back to your lady tonight? Is she waiting in your bed?'

'No …?' he said, his tone a question.

'So, we don't have a problem then!' When he didn't seem convinced, she elaborated. 'Look, it doesn't matter, okay?

Linear timelines are a bitch. If it helps, just think about the time we spend together tonight in a vacuum. Let's say, one … two hours?' She looked him up and down, as if estimating his sexual abilities just by his outward appearances.

'Two hours,' he blurted out defensively.

'Okay, tiger. Two hours. If it helps you, just imagine that these two hours happened before you met your lady. In any case, what difference does it make to her, how you spend these two hours of your life? You could be sitting here, drinking. You could be in your bed, sleeping. You could be with me, having an experience of a lifetime.'

'That's not how monogamy works. This is cheating,' Ravi argued meekly.

'Cheating? Life isn't a game!' she chortled.

'It's just how it is. That's how things work. I didn't make the rules!'

'Rules? Humans crack me up.' *Why did she say it like that? Humans. Like she wasn't one?* She continued, a tinge more seriously, 'Listen, it's up to you. It is unlikely we are ever going to see each other again. I'm hardly going to be a constant presence in your life, coming between you and your lady. No one would ever know.'

'Someone might find out.'

'So, *that's* what you're afraid of? You're not afraid of doing the deed. You're worried about someone finding out!'

This time, Ravi didn't defend himself. It was useless anyway.

'Well, if that's all you're worried about, what if I promise you that no one would know? We'll make sure of it. Why don't you tell me your room number and I'll go there first?

You can meet me in a few minutes, separately. How would they know? It can be our little secret adventure. I mean, come on, did you have anything better planned tonight? Why waste the night?'

Why indeed, Ravi concluded. He slid his room key across the bar counter towards her. She picked it up, made a show of waving him goodbye, and disappeared.

Ravi reclaimed his stool. He sat at the edge of his seat, his head resting heavily in his hands, his elbows digging into the bar counter. Anyone who observed his interaction with her could clearly see that she had left, waving goodbye and he remained. He bid his time, as his heart beat loudly in his ears, drowning out the *thump thump* of EDM. He didn't know who she was, where she came from or what she wanted with him, but he decided to go along for the ride.

Ravi took small, calculated steps out of the elevator. He paused in front of the door to his suite, looked both ways to check if someone was watching him. The hallway was deserted. He lifted his fist to knock on the suite door, but it was pulled open before his knuckles made contact with the wood.

A slim arm with long, green fingernails appeared. She grabbed hold of his collar and pulled him inside. In the darkness, she pushed him against the closed door, with determined force. In one swift motion, she ran her fingers down his shirt, which flew open, buttons landing on the carpeted floor soundlessly.

'Mmm,' she whispered as she spread open his shirt and nestled her face in his chest. She breathed him in. Ran her fingers through his hair. She kissed him gently, the softness a contrast against everything her fervent hands did to his body. She launched herself upwards, climbing on him, relying on him to catch her.

And he did. He snaked his arms around her tight little body, held her to him. He carried her to the bed, threw her on it. He climbed on top of her. Pushed the cloud of pink hair that covered her face. Her green eyes shone in the dark. He kissed her neck, her collarbone, her breasts. His mouth was tender, his hands restless, making their way up under her dress.

She moaned. She let him pin her down, overpower her. She made sweet, soft sounds of arousal that drove him crazy. She murmured in his ear, told him what she wanted him to do to her. She thanked him. She asked for more. She did everything Avani didn't do anymore. Avani only cared about her own pleasure, but this girl ... She surrendered herself to him.

She was okay with him being in control. With him lifting her up, throwing her around. With him taking, getting his way. He didn't have to try hard to push thoughts of Avani out of his mind. This girl was the opposite of everything Avani was. She was everything he wanted. And he had her.

He had every inch of her.

🌹

Ravi's eyes flew open. The room swam in front of his blurry eyes. It was dark. He could still smell her, but when he ran his hands on the bed on either side of him, it was empty, cold.

Everything was cold. The entire room was freezing. His toes were stiff in the cold wind that entered through the open window, alight in the glow of the moonlight. In the frame of the window, he made out the silhouette of her naked body.

'Aren't you freezing …?' he muttered. The sound didn't make it out of his lips. It was caught somewhere in his throat. He tried again. 'What are you doing?'

She was perched on the windowsill, balanced precariously on the tips of her toes. She wore nothing but her smile. She looked towards him for a moment, then turned away again. Her bare body swayed in the wind as she made to get up, as if to fly.

Ravi felt terror rise in his chest. Alarmed, he screamed in the dark, 'What are you doing?' These words also failed to make it out of his mouth. No matter how hard he tried, the sound kept getting caught in his throat.

He watched in horror as she switched to a crouching position, as if to ready-set-go, and before he could get up and stop her, she jumped.

Ravi's body convulsed in horror. This time, one word finally escaped his mouth, but it was far too late. 'Stop!'

The sound of his own voice screaming 'Stop!' jolted Ravi from his sleep. His foot lost balance and slipped out of the footrest of his stool. He looked around. He was in the club, still alight in purple and pink. The music was a low hum. Ravi was one of the handful of people remaining.

'You all right, man?' the bartender asked.

Ravi balanced himself by leaning against the bar counter. Of course, he had passed out here after nine whiskies and dreamed a vivid dream about a pink-haired fairy with green eyes. That scenario made sense – more than that of the hot night they shared together, and her jumping out of the window, or flying, or whatever it was that she had done. He was relieved that she wasn't a supernatural creature who had flown away after having sex with him, or a regular human girl who, post-coitus, had jumped out of the window. Neither of those scenarios were ideal.

'Yeah, yeah,' he said, collecting himself. It was the same bartender who had served him all night. Ravi asked, 'Hey, did you happen to ... Was there a girl there?' He pointed across the bar. 'Pink hair, big eyes.'

The bartender looked at him unsurely. 'I don't know who you're talking about ...'

'She was sitting over there? Short and really pretty. Like a fairy,' Ravi blurted out, cursing himself for sounding so desperate.

'I don't know.' When Ravi's face fell, the bartender added, giving him some hope, 'But maybe. It's possible. I was on my break for the last one hour or so ...'

'Never mind,' Ravi said hastily. He pulled out his credit card and offered it to the bartender.

'I can just charge it to your room if you prefer. You're the groom, no?'

Ravi regretted saying anything about the imaginary fairy to this stranger who knew he was about to get married. 'Yes, thanks.' He pocketed his card and turned to leave. He couldn't help himself from turning around and adding, 'It's nothing like that, by the way. The girl … She was just … Like, nothing's going on or anything.'

'Of course, sir.' The bartender's face was completely blank, but Ravi could sense the judgement under his professional demeanour.

'It's anyway none of your business. Just keep your mouth shut,' he spat out and left.

He stumbled towards his suite. On his way, he passed the room his friends and cousins had chosen to throw the strip party at. The door was left ajar, the lights on. Ravi poked his head inside. Music was playing softly while his friends and cousins lay around the room, on the bed, the carpet, the couch, like discarded articles of clothing. Upon very little inspection, Ravi discovered actual discarded articles of clothing too. An impossibly small G-string, tassels, glitter and empty shot glasses in the shape of boobs adorned the floor.

Ravi shook his head at their stupidity and shut the front door behind him, looking for a place to pass out with his dumb friends and cousins. 'Idiots,' he muttered to himself, smiling. He was in a surprisingly great mood, for someone as tired as he was. His friends sure did have fun, but, most likely, not as much as Ravi had had in his dreams.

Ravi fell face first on an unoccupied side of the bed. He couldn't wait to conjure her up again, relive his fantasy. His new reality wouldn't be so bad if he was capable of fabricating such vivid dreams every once in a while.

🌹

Avani wasn't happy about the swollen faces and under-eye bags, betraying the late-night exploits of her groom and his stag party. After some sweet-talking, Ravi was able to manage her foul mood. This was what he liked about the fairy. She was capable, came without baggage, needed no managing. And still, in the bedroom, she was the perfect submissive princess he fancied.

It was unfair of him to compare a real person, his bride-to-be, to his fantasy, Ravi knew that. He couldn't help it. Avani could lock him up, monitor all his actions, like she had done for years, since she found out about his other exploits. But she couldn't govern his thoughts. They were his own. They could be as wild as his heart desired.

🌹

Ravi looked up at Avani. In her magenta bridal clothes, she was a sight to behold. It was sure to make a splash on social media. Watching him watch her, she smiled at him. He smiled back. At least five cameras were trained on them. Everyone was watching them. There was a sudden rise in the incessant chatter around them. It was time for the *varmala*, the garland exchange.

All their friends climbed up on the stage and surrounded them. Ravi was thumped on his back, something his cousins loved to do as a sign of celebration. They weren't so much with the words. He was handed a garland, and so was Avani. He looked up at her. What he saw next made him catch his breath.

Pink hair. Green eyes. The fairy. She was real. She was standing next to Avani. He stood frozen to the spot. She met his eyes unabashedly, clearly sensing his anxiety. Her face stretched into a big smile. She was still every bit as stunning as she had been the night before, but … in a more human sort of way. Without the purple and pink flashing lights, without the candle light reflecting on her lip gloss, without the curtain of loud music, the whisky.

Ravi gulped. He went through the motions, doing as was instructed. He exchanged garlands with Avani, smiled for the camera. He shook hands, hugged, touched feet. All the while replaying everything that had happened the previous night. How much of it was a dream? What had really happened? Had he really cheated on his bride the night before their wedding? Was her friend going to tell Avani what had happened? If so, wouldn't she have done it before the varmala exchange? What was she doing here? He had to put all the questions on hold and put on a show for the hundreds of guests who had collected to watch them. He felt like an animal, trapped behind bars in a zoo. Everyone wanted his attention.

Later, much later, he spotted pink hair in the crowd. He disengaged from his group as unsuspiciously as he could and sneaked up to her. 'What … who?' he blabbered. For some reason, he could never seem to form full sentences when he was around her.

She smiled. There was no sweetness to it. It was a smirk, bitter and victorious. 'I couldn't find a room,' she stated simply. 'I got time-off at the last minute, and didn't want to miss Avani's wedding. I flew in, but the resort was fully booked. And I knew you had one of the best rooms. So, I took it from you. Embarrassing how easy it was.'

Ravi's expression betrayed the hurt he felt.

She shrugged. 'Oh, come on! I don't feel bad for you one bit. I told myself that if I flirted with you and you didn't stop me, *the night before marrying my friend,* you deserved your room to be stolen. I must admit, though, I had expected you to come knocking on the door. I was looking forward to turning you away. It's not like you could've told anyone. What would you have said? That you willingly gave your key to a girl you were going to sleep with the night before your wedding? But you never came. What happened? Did you, like, pass out at the bar?'

Ravi looked down shamefacedly.

She burst out laughing, a vile, spiteful sound. 'You *did*? I can't believe it. This keeps getting better and better. A story for a lifetime.'

With that, she sashayed away.

Ravi reeled with the impact of the new revelations. This explained why he hadn't been able to find his key card in the morning and had to get a new one from the reception. His dreams, his fantasies, were a result not only of the whisky, but also her targeted flirtation. He was furious to have been toyed with, deceived like this. But she was right. Who could he tell? What would they say?

He rejoined his bride on the stage. Now that he thought of it, didn't Avani say that her flight attendant friend, the one with the Swiss father and Brazilian mother, might make it to the wedding last minute? She had told him about the green eyes, but the pink hair was a surprise. And he had taken her ethnically ambiguous appearance to mean that she was … a fairy. This was humiliating.

No matter how he tried to spin it, see it in a positive light, it failed to make him feel better. The only positive was that at least he didn't start his married life by cheating on his wife the night before the wedding. That didn't really make him feel better, because they had been married secretly for two years; this wedding was just for show. Their relationship was a sham, barely held together by the weakest of threads.

Most of all, he was furious that his fantasy had been taken away from him, without which, he had an eternity of only his real, miserable life to look forward to.

MAMABEAR

I don't want to be like this. No one wants to be like this. But I don't have a choice. Uptight, scared, paranoid. I know the names they call me behind my back. My entire family and all my friends. Even my husband.

Maybe not my husband, actually (but I can never be sure what he talks about with his mother and sister; every time one of them calls, he always walks away for a few minutes). He was there with me. He knows what it was like. How terrifying it was to give birth to our first child during the peak of a pandemic. The word everyone uses *for these difficult times* is 'unprecedented'. Our experience warrants that overused, domesticated word. When I think back to the week I gave birth, I shiver. Even now, it feels surreal.

To have survived something like that feels like a miracle in itself. I don't consider myself much of a religious, or even spiritual, person. And yet, experiences like these have the power to change you, make you want to believe ... in something. A higher power of sorts. Someone competent in charge. I've been the type of Hindu who only *feels* Hindu during festivals. Celebrating Holi, Diwali and Durga Puja every year with my family has brought me a joy I've always taken for granted. This year, we've skipped all the festivals, along with everything else.

Coronavirus crept into our country in March. I had seen it coming, because I had been *reading* the news diligently. Emphasis on reading. Not watching poorly produced video clips forwarded via WhatsApp groups or shared by long-lost acquaintances on Facebook. With the arrival of this novel virus, denial, conspiracy theories and natural remedies ran rampant throughout the nation. My own father ordered Arsenic Album 30 on Amazon and had it delivered to my doorstep. I was nine months pregnant then, and he expected me to take a foreign substance I knew nothing about, backed by no scientific research or evidence, and run the risk of poisoning my unborn baby! Pratham, ever the dutiful son-in-law, decided to try out the three-day course of Papa's homoeopathic prescription just to placate him. A little too eager to please, in my opinion. I, however, was in open rebellion. Ever since Google first became a household necessity, I have had the superpower to challenge every single one of my father's baseless claims about things he knows very little about but professes to know a lot about. Our heated but friendly arguments have been the backbone of our loving relationship. On this particular issue, in the end, we agreed to disagree. I had no interest in continuing the conversation. I was a little distracted by my contractions.

Like I was saying, I don't care if my family and friends think I am uptight, scared or paranoid. They weren't there. They don't understand where I'm coming from. The week I delivered Alia defines and validates how seriously we take the coronavirus. When I tell you, you'll understand too.

Day 1:

I was still in bed, sipping the Darjeeling chai Pratham had made for us when I went into labour. I was watching my caffeine intake, allowing myself a cup of chai in the morning for the sake of sanity. It was mid-April, the entire country was under lockdown. The first twenty-one-day lockdown period was about to end, but the Maharashtra government had already announced a second phase. This, for us, meant that neither my parents nor Pratham's could be with us for the delivery of their first grandchild. We had made our peace with that, a bit unhealthily, by pushing it under the rug and not thinking about it. There was nothing we could do about it anyway.

For a few days there, right before I went into labour, it seemed like our hospital wouldn't even allow Pratham to be with me during delivery. Fortunately, that didn't end up happening. Both of us had to take the COVID-19 test upon arrival at the hospital. Both our tests were fast-tracked, but only I was cleared to go in immediately, given that I was in labour. While the results were awaited, Pratham wasn't allowed to accompany me inside. He waited in the parking lot, in the April heat, with the sun beating down on our car, for eight hours.

Meanwhile, I went from counter to counter, filling out mandatory forms. I was in so much pain that I could neither sit nor stand. No nurse was willing to help me. They maintained distance from me, in their PPE, stepping backwards if I approached them. I was shown to a room where I was promptly abandoned. Hours later, when my test came back negative, a nurse finally took pity on me and helped me tie my gown; my hands couldn't reach that far back, so before this kind nurse's intervention, I had been pacing around my room like a whale in agony, my gown slipping off my naked body every few minutes. Every time that happened, it took me immense effort to crouch down and pick it up, poke my arms through the holes, attempt to tie the strings behind my back, fail, repeat.

Day 2:

It was clear to my gynaecologist, after twenty-nine hours of labour, that I couldn't give birth naturally. Pratham was with me, in PPE, his arm snaked around my shoulders to help me sit up on the hospital bed, when we were told that a Caesarean section was in order.

Moments later, I was wheeled away from my husband. In that instant, I felt so inadequate; I had failed to perform a simple task that was expected of my body, and I had wasted twenty-nine hours trying. The nurses had made it abundantly clear during those twenty-nine hours, every time I had pressed the button on my bedside, terrified that something was wrong, that they were needed elsewhere, that there was a pandemic, that I was behaving like a spoiled brat.

All that, just to ultimately be taken to the operation theatre, where more of their precious time was demanded, when there were women around the world, even in fully developed countries, giving birth in their own homes, without seeking so much unwarranted attention from important people who had other matters to attend to.

Most of all, my heart broke at the look on Pratham's face, watching me getting wheeled away to an operation theatre, once again left alone, on the outside, when we had always dreamed of bringing our baby into this world together.

'Come back ...' he had whispered desperately, squeezing my hand in both of his. We had approached the door. He couldn't go any further. His eyes were wild.

'I'm not ... I'm not dying or anything.' I forced a chuckle. It didn't work. My throat was dry; every atom of my being filled with fear. For my baby, for my husband, for me, for our family.

The nurses, once again, didn't care about our family drama. 'We have to go,' one of them said curtly.

'I'll come back,' I said quickly to Pratham.

'I love you so much. So, so much.' And then, he let go of my hand. He was crying. He was broken, helpless. I was taken away. I forgot all about my pain, about the existence of my body. Please don't let me die, *I prayed to the competent, higher power in charge.*

Day 3:

The hospital kept me and Alia for twenty-four hours after her birth, for observation. Only, there was hardly anyone observing us. The nurses hadn't even cleaned me after the surgery. They had cleaned the incisions immediately after the C-section, of course, but hadn't returned to check on them since. No one helped me breastfeed Alia for the very first time.

The hospital kicked Pratham out two hours after the delivery. Once again, he stood on the outside of his family, completely incapable of contributing. He returned home alone, leaving his family to fend for themselves. I kept my phone plugged in, call connected to Pratham. We had him there in the cold hospital bed, in a small but immensely comforting way.

I didn't sleep a wink that first night, didn't look away from Alia's small, pink face even once. Something had changed in me the moment she was born. I stopped being timid, apologetic. This was my baby, and she needed me to be her advocate. She was helpless without me, and her only hope for survival was my vigilance. So, I made noise.

When, two hours before my discharge, the gynaecologist still hadn't checked in on us, I called the nurses till they gave in. When they told me that I was free to go, I made them roll me and Alia out to the front – in my wheelchair and Alia's stroller – where Pratham was waiting for us. Despite the popular opinion in that hospital, I wasn't being a spoiled brat. I was terrified. Of my stitched-up belly bursting open, of my trembling hands dropping my baby. Of how slippery the floors looked, how wobbly my insides felt.

Nothing felt safe. I had my baby to protect now. Overnight, I had fully transformed into a mama bear.

Day 4:

If you thought the worst was behind us, you were wrong. No, we didn't get COVID-19, but the day after we brought Alia home, I got a fever. My temperature went up as high as 105° Fahrenheit. While I insisted that I was fine, Pratham was

terrified. I was more terrified of going back to the hospital.
He begged me to let him take me to the doctor. His tactics
were terrible; he tried to convince me by building horrifying
hypothetical scenarios where he's left alone with Alia. He
painted a heart-wrenching picture of father and daughter
going through life together, without me.

In the end, I agreed to have someone from the hospital
come over to examine me and take a COVID test. There was
no way I was going back to the hospital. I don't know how
Pratham managed to pull it off, with the shortage of medical
professionals all across the city, but, a few hours later, a nurse
appeared at our door.

That night, I still had a fever, I still hadn't slept since I
gave birth, but I was home with my family. I had taken the
over-the-counter medication the nurse had prescribed, and
while my body was still warm, it was nowhere as hot as
earlier that day. We video called our parents on WhatsApp,
and, for an instant, I could see things going back to normal
from that moment forward. It was when I picked up Alia
for her bedtime feed that I realized her body was burning
hotter than mine.

Day 5:

After another sleepless night of staring at my daughter's face
in a cold hospital bed, I was told that we were free to go. Only,
I didn't want to. My baby had jaundice. Yes, her fever was
gone, but that was only because of the doctor's attention and
phototherapy. At home, we didn't have those things. I wanted
to scream at them, shake them into understanding that this

baby's parents were not equipped for this. That we had no help, and we couldn't be trusted to keep our baby alive.

I did exactly that. I broke down completely and created a scene, peered into every face hidden behind N-95 masks, forcing them to see me, understand me. That stunt got me a few more hours in the hospital. By the time we were discharged, Alia looked healthier, but my fever was raging.

That night, despite myself, my body took over, putting my mind under. I slept for the first time in seventy-two hours.

Day 6:

When I woke up, Pratham had Alia ready for her feed. He had bathed her, clothed her and swaddled her in the furry green blanket my mother had sent us. In the morning light, our baby looked so precious. Pratham handled her with such care, laying her carefully in my arms, the way he had been doing in the middle of the night, when I was asleep and Alia needed to eat. He had held her in position the entire time, letting me sleep.

Now, as I fed her again, cradling her in my arms, emotions welled up in my chest.

'You are my whole world,' Pratham said with such sincerity, looking at me and our daughter, that my body jerked with tears. Having a baby felt like our armour had been taken away. We became naked now, soft and defenceless.

All I could do was nod, as I touched his cheek, thanking God for my family. I still didn't quite understand religion, didn't believe in God, and my fever still wasn't gone, but somehow, *in that moment, I needed to have faith in something … faith that we would be okay.*

Now, when our families joke – light-heartedly, but with intention – about us being too strict, too precious with our baby, I don't let it get to me. I'm her mother, her advocate. I have had to go to the hospital several times in the six months since Alia's birth, for her vaccines and my check-ups. I have seen first-hand how bad the coronavirus can get, how overwhelmed the healthcare system is. I check the numbers of cases every single day. The graphs continue their upward curve; yet, the entire population simply ignores the scientific facts and data.

Every day, more people die, while our cousins pressure us to let them hold our baby. It's not like we haven't allowed anyone near Alia. We really have done the absolute most that we can do, while still being safe. Once, we took Alia outside in her stroller to meet our friends. Yes, we told them beforehand that they had to keep their masks on and stay six-feet away from us – but those are basic precautions that we're all supposed to take, all across the planet.

We order our groceries online and cook our meals at home, because that way, we can wash everything beforehand. We even ordered a gentle, organic soap, especially made to wash fruits and vegetables with. Of course, every time we receive a delivery – other than perishables – we leave the packages at the entrance, by the door, for fourteen days before opening them. Then, we wipe everything with disinfectant before bringing them inside. We sanitize our shoes after we have been outside, and, in the off-chance that we order from a restaurant, we order food that can be put directly into the oven at a high temperature for five minutes, just to be safe.

I know that our precautions seem extreme to others, but every time I imagine something bad happening, it ensures me that we are doing the right thing. How would we feel if something were to happen to any of us, just because we had a craving for pizza?

Four months after Alia was born, we finally felt comfortable enough to introduce her to both sets of grandparents. Of course, since they took flights to visit us, we asked them to quarantine at a hotel for fourteen days first, get tested on day one and then again on day fourteen, and then come to our home. When they did, we had them go straight to the bathroom, take baths and change into fresh clothes before holding Alia. It seemed like a lot when we explained the precautions to them, but, in the end, wasn't it worth it, for them to hold their first grandchild?

❦

'This can't be right ...' I say out loud, to myself. 'There's no way. *Pratham!*'

'Nina? Did you say something?' Pratham calls from the bedroom, where he and his parents are playing with Alia on her half-birthday. My parents had returned home after a month, declaring that there really wasn't enough room for all of us in our small apartment, not when no one was allowed to go outside for a walk without having to go straight to the bathroom to take a bath afterwards. I know that they cared less about the small space and more about our perfectly justified precautions.

'Can you come here?' I call back. My voice is shaky. I reread the email. When Pratham appears, I shove my phone in his face. 'Have you seen this email? I was looking for Alia's medical records to check what other vaccines she needs when I found this ...'

As Pratham reads, his brows furrow. I watch him go through the same set of emotions I had gone through mere moments ago.

I breathe in disbelief. 'How is this possible? How could we miss this? This email wasn't unread. I must've opened it when I was half-asleep or something ...'

'This is dated 2 May. What were we doing then?' Pratham searches my eyes.

'We were probably dead tired. Alia was less than a month old! We had no idea what we were doing! But, like, shouldn't the hospital have called us? I don't remember getting a call. Did *you* get a call?'

'We definitely missed some calls in the first month ... We missed a lot of things! Like this email ...'

Pratham and I look at each other, our eyes wide. Our hospital had emailed me a positive COVID-19 test result roughly three weeks after I delivered Alia, and we never saw it. We either missed their phone calls, or the hospital didn't call us, due to oversight or the incompetence of their overworked staff.

I take the phone back from Pratham and stare at the email. I can't believe that after everything we have done in the last six months to protect our family from COVID-19, it turns out that I already had COVID-19 and didn't know about it. That while we quarantined diligently, insulating ourselves, and our baby, from the outside world, the virus had been in our home all along, quiet, undetected.

NATASHA

Gautam's phone vibrated in his pocket. He didn't have to check it to know that it was Natasha. This was the third time she had called today. He had picked up the first time, right before an important meeting, but had to let the second call go to voicemail. This time, he grew concerned. She never called him twice, without giving him a chance to call her back in-between calls. She knew he always called her as soon as he got a free moment.

His gut told him something was wrong. He gulped and tried not to panic. Not before he found a cause for panic, at least. He turned to the room and said, 'Excuse me, guys. I have to take this.'

The two other men in the room, sitting on either side of him around the large conference table, looked at him and nodded shortly. 'Sure,' one of them said.

Gautam slipped out through the glass door and took the call. 'Natasha? Is everything okay?' He tried and failed to keep the panic out of his voice.

'Gautam? Gautam, please come home,' Natasha sobbed on the other side.

'What happened? Are you okay?' Gautam's heart began to thud wildly in his chest.

'I'm ... I'm ... not.'

'What is it? Do you need medical help? Are you bleeding?'

'Yes ...' Natasha's voice was shaky, barely audible.

There was a pause, during which a hundred horrifying pictures ran through Gautam's mind. Some imagined, others from memory. He never should've left her alone. He knew deep within that something like this would happen. He had felt a premonition somewhere within him, but had brushed it off as paranoia. Just because it had happened once didn't mean it had to happen again. They'd come across terrible luck in the past year, but things had been looking better. He never should've left her alone. How many times had she begged him to be with her? Why didn't he just stay?

'Tasha ...' he murmured, and the questions came pouring out of him. 'What happened? How did this happen?'

'I ...' Natasha sobbed. Her voice sounded muffled, as if she was speaking through layers of fabric. 'I was cooking ... I was chopping tomatoes ... My bad arm. It just ... Suddenly, there was so much blood everywhere.'

'Out of the blue? I don't understand—'

'Come home, Gautam. Please, I need you ...'

'Yes, yes, I'm coming. How much blood ... is it worse than before? Were you in the – hello? Hello? Are you there? Natasha?'

There were three sharp beeps, and then nothing. Gautam immediately called back her number. It went straight to voicemail. Had she hung up by accident? Had her phone died?

Was she losing more blood? He couldn't let panic overwhelm him. He had to fix this. He had to save her. She had endured enough.

He moved swiftly. First, he called 911 and gave the operator whatever little information he had and their address. Then, he swung by the conference room to say, 'I have to go home. My wife. There's a medical emergency.' His co-workers looked at him with wide eyes for a short second, then nodded fervently. Gautam was already gone.

❀

Falguni placed her phone face down on the couch. Then, she flung the fridge door open and poked her head in. The cool air felt nice on her warm face. She could feel her ears burning. She didn't have to look in a mirror to know that they were flushed red. She snatched the bottle of orange juice and slammed the door shut.

Her breath came in gasps. Gautam would be here soon.

She slipped to the floor, leaning against the fridge. How did this happen? How did they get here? She only sat there, on the floor, for a few minutes, but it felt like hours. Time had lost its meaning. In the short while that Falguni sat on the floor, eyes closed, head resting against the fridge door, clutching a bottle of orange juice, she relived years of her life … everything that had led to this moment, all came rushing back to her.

❀

She was only twenty-two when her father got the phone call from Arun Uncle, presenting him with the *rishta*, the proposal. Arun Uncle's sister-in-law's brother was an NRI, living in New York and earning a salary of over ₹1 crore per year. That was all they knew at first. A few days on, Gautam's photo was forwarded to Falguni's father over WhatsApp.

Falguni had thrown a tantrum, created a scene in front of everyone in revolt.

'I don't want to get married!' she cried.

Her chachis and chachas had glared at her. So had her dada and dadi. But she knew she had her parents' sympathy, counting on which, she pressed on. 'Papa, please. *Bas ek saal aur*. All I ask for is another year. Why are you rushing like this? I'm only twenty—'

'Wait for what?' her older cousin had interjected. Gulab Bhaiya was always butting his head in other people's business where it didn't belong.

'I … I want to study more!' Falguni pulled that one out of thin air. She had no interest in further education, but she said what every other young girl in the country resorted to, to delay an impending arranged marriage.

'Oh-ho-ho! *Now* you want to study? Then why have you not been doing it since last year, instead of just sitting at home useless?'

'I needed a break! I didn't know what I wanted!'

'And now you do?' her chachi challenged.

'Umm … I want to be a teacher. I want to do a B.Ed. or maybe fill forms for bank jobs,' Falguni said desperately.

'Those are two *very* different things,' Gulab Bhaiya declared victoriously. 'You have no idea what you want to do with your life—'

'I know that I don't want to get married! Just give me one more year, Papa.' Falguni turned to her father and pleaded, her voice low, cajoling. 'What's the rush? Please! There's no reason to rush—'

'Gunnu,' her father said. His tone was different than what she had expected. More stoic. It stilled something in her. '*Bas. Bohot ho gaya.* Enough!'

His voice sent shivers down her spine. 'Papa, please,' she braved a last meek attempt.

The slap across her face threw her to the ground. The sting caused tears to pour freely out of her eyes. Her entire body shook. No one moved. No one said anything. No one came to help her get up. The shock and betrayal hurt more than the part of her cheek that had connected with the back of her father's hand. She was confused, confounded. What had just happened? Why? She had heard horror stories from her friends about their fathers, but her own father wasn't that type of a man.

She looked from one frozen face to another. They were all looking at her. Yet, there was absolute silence. 'Kya ...?' she began, but courage deserted her. Her mind raced. What did they know? Who told them? What was going to happen to her? Would she never see Manoj again? Would he find her?

Falguni picked herself up from the floor. Her pride stopped herself from touching her face. All 5'2" of her slight frame stood tall. Her eyes travelled to every face in the room. No one spoke. They stood there, gathered in the dining room. Her younger cousins put their heads down and pretended to do their homework at the dining table. Her dada sat in front of the TV in the drawing room, with his back turned to them. Her dadi looked on from the kitchen door.

Breathing heavily, Falguni stomped towards the room she shared with her younger brother. When she walked by her father, he held out an arm to stop her.

'You think we are blind idiots?' He was breathing heavily, and his voice came out in a snarl. 'Gulab told us everything. We are accepting Arun's rishta. You are going to marry Gautam and go to America. You're going to forget all about this Manoj character. And, till then, you are not to leave the house alone. Understood?'

Falguni's face burned. Fresh, hot tears flowed down her throbbing cheek. In embarrassment, in pain, in horror. In a matter of minutes, her life had crashed down around her.

The decision to change her name was her cousin's brilliant idea. According to him, Falguni sounded too gawar, too 'villager-like'. As far as status went, she was marrying up. Which meant she needed to act the part, starting with her name. Natasha Thakur sounded far classier than Falguni Kumari. Once she was married, she would get a fresh start in life. All traces of Falguni Kumari from Daltonganj, Jharkhand, would be erased.

This was important to the rest of her family too. Ever since the local newspaper printed articles about Falguni Kumari attempting to elope with a farmer's son, Manoj Shankar, Falguni's family had been obsessed with erasing all of her past life, put it behind them and move on.

Falguni couldn't protest; she had lost all her power. Now, she was assigned the role of the perfect porcelain doll: stay silent, look pretty, be discarded from her family and sent to another.

After the wedding, Gautam promptly returned to New York. He had only been able to get two weeks off from work, for his own wedding, a fact that was brought up and commented upon by relatives on both sides at the ceremony. The most that Falguni and Gautam had spoken to each other was at the wedding reception, during which they sat in garish red velvet wing armchairs placed next to each other, at the centre of a makeshift stage. They were on display like that for four hours. People neither of them knew came up on the stage, and Falguni and Gautam would share a look to communicate if the newest guests they had the honour to welcome looked older than the bride and groom, and, if they did, they bent down and touched their feet. If not, they would bring their palms together, bow their heads and say, '*Namaste ji.*'

It almost became a game, during which Falguni built a certain camaraderie with Gautam. Maybe this marriage wasn't going to be as terrible as she had imagined. Then again, she spotted Manoj by the chow mein stand, standing still with his friend Pankaj, his eyes fixed on her. When their eyes met, Falguni was transported out of her body, to a hot summer day under a bushy tree, tucked away in the shade, his sweat rubbing on to her skin, her lips parted, his mouth on her breast.

❧

Before she could follow her new husband to New York, Falguni lived with Gautam's family for six months in Gaya. The process of getting a passport and a visa was time-consuming.

There, she built a surprisingly strong friendship with Gautam's younger sister, Garima. She learned a lot about her new family from her. Garima was in her final year of college, and was far more modern than Falguni and her friends back in Daltonganj. For instance, she was allowed to wear jeans with her kurta, even without a dupatta. Some of Garima's friends were male and were even invited to their house often. Falguni brought chai and snacks to them in the drawing room, going from one person to the next, holding out the tray. She would stand by the door and listen to them talk, uninhibited. This wasn't a family of secrets.

'Don't your parents mind these boys coming to the house?' Falguni once asked, keeping her voice low as she stirred the pot of dal.

'Of course not! They're not backward like that!' Garima said. She was perched on the counter, her legs dangling playfully. 'You don't have to worry either, Bhabhi. I know your parents were very strict, but you're in our family now. As soon as your visa comes, you'll fly to join Bhaiya in New York. Forget about all those rules in Daltonganj. Who cares?'

Falguni was too scared to hope, but the thought of her family never being able to put a hand on her again brought a smile to her lips.

'And who knows? I'll join you in New York soon too! I'm applying to universities there. I'll keep trying till I get in. You could even do it with me! We can be successful career women one day. Just leave all of this behind.' There was a contagious spark in Garima's eyes.

Falguni felt something in her chest loosen.

When Falguni finally made it to New York, she wasn't as overwhelmed as she had feared she would be. Garima had prepared her well. They'd watched all ten seasons of *Friends* on Garima's laptop with English subtitles on, to facilitate her understanding of the American accent. Falguni's education had been in Hindi medium; so even though she could read English, her spoken English needed a lot of work. Garima was fluent in the foreign language and took pride in helping her sister-in-law.

Once in New York, Falguni really missed Garima's friendship. She had grown accustomed to her warmth and humour. They still spoke through WhatsApp video calls, but the ten-and-a-half-hour time difference made it difficult to stay connected the way they had been in Gaya.

Now, Falguni was on her own, trying to learn who her husband was. The first thing she noticed about Gautam was that he was ... balding. It was evident now due to the absence of the groom's *sehra* from his head. Also, in the brief time he had spent in India after their wedding, he had always worn a cap, even indoors. Outdoors, he wore dark black sunglasses that made him look blind. It was as though he had never seen the sun before in his life.

Gautam was a man of routine. He woke up at the same time every morning, took a shower, put on his work clothes that he had ironed and hung on the back of the door the night before, ate cereal in 2 per cent fat milk and took the subway to his office. He came home at the same time every evening, and Falguni had dinner ready. They ate together, he called home, and they watched TV for an hour before bed.

The problem was: he didn't sleep in the bed with her. Every night, he took the time to lower the back of the couch to lay it flat, stretched out a fitted bedsheet around the edges, topped it with a flat sheet and a blanket, and pulled the curtains to make the living room blackout dark. In the morning, he meticulously undid the entire set up, only to do it all over again at night.

At first, Falguni was relieved, the same way she had been on their wedding night, when he'd told her she could sleep on the bed and he slept on the floor out of respect for her privacy. They had been strangers, after all. However, after being married for nine months, and living together for three months, Falguni found it deeply unsettling that he didn't share the bed with her.

She wasn't physically attracted to him. He wore old-man spectacles. He wasn't very tall either. He had dry patches around his eyes and wore lifts in his shoes when he went to work, adding two inches to his 5'7" frame. She couldn't help but compare him to Manoj, who used to work in a farm and had the firm body of a farmer. He had no extra fat on his body, which moved like well-oiled machinery. So, this soft, stout man was hardly stirring desire in her. But what else was there to do?

Falguni's days had begun to resemble one another. They lived in downtown Manhattan because Gautam wanted to experience the vibrant energy of the place, opting for it over the comfort and familiarity of Jersey City, with its many Indian grocery stores, restaurants and people. Falguni had to learn to order Indian groceries online. She had even learned to cook pasta from Garima over a WhatsApp video call. Once Falguni learned how to use Gautam's iPad to search for recipes on YouTube, she didn't look back. Every day, she tried to cook something new. Every week, they ordered different groceries, venturing more and more into territories foreign to her.

After three months of it, she had grown tired. Gautam was still appreciative of her efforts, but seeing as Falguni's only role in his life was to cook and clean for him, she felt like his maid. Sex could change that.

She found herself smelling his shirts before washing them, craving his touch. One night, after tossing and turning in the cold bed for an hour, she sat up, pushed the covers back and decided it was time for her to take action. She rose and padded to the living room. She left the lights off, as she walked over to the couch. Gautam turned over and looked up at her in the dark room.

'What's wrong?' he whispered.

'You are my husband,' Falguni said. She lowered herself to the floor, on her knees to meet his eyes.

'Natasha …' Gautam muttered.

Falguni leaned forward and placed her lips firmly on his. His mouth smelled like peppermint and his body smelled like his dirty shirts. She pressed harder. Lifting her head to look at him, she lowered it again for another kiss. Without breaking it, she climbed on top of the couch, on top of him. Their bodies were separated by the blanket.

Gautam didn't make any sounds, but his hands were now clasped around her. They slid lower, to her hips, of which he grabbed a handful. His grip on her hardened, when she slipped her fingers under the blanket and reached for his pants. He was kissing her back now, his tongue exploring hers. Their breath became one.

Soon, they were up on their feet, peeling off their clothes. Gautam threw the blanket to the floor and they got back on his couch–bed. His breathing was more haggard now. *Too haggard*, Falguni observed. Soon after, *too soon*, he lay on his back, panting hard, finished.

🌹

After that night, the couch wasn't made into a bed again. Gautam slept with Falguni in the bedroom. As relieved as

Falguni was to have a normal marriage, she couldn't help but feel disgusted by how quickly he finished every time. How short, and frankly boring, their sex was. Always in the bed, always in the same position, always finished within minutes.

In a few months, Gautam lost interest too. They still did it once a week, like clockwork, more as an obligation than for pleasure or connection.

It was nothing like Manoj's tight, sweaty body ramming into her. Falguni missed how hungrily Manoj used to suck on her breasts, how aggressively he shoved his fingers inside her, how hard he slapped her face, how disgusting the names he called her were. She tried to forget about him, pushed those memories away every time they resurfaced. They kept coming up at the most inconvenient of times. Like now, as she watched Gautam carefully pick up his cup and slurp his chai, the image of Manoj's laughing face as he repositioned her so Pankaj could push deeper inside her, flashed before her eyes.

In her hometown, it had been difficult for Falguni and Manoj to find a discreet place to be together. Pankaj had provided that secret place for them. He had only been half-joking when he said he wanted a taste of her in exchange. Later, Manoj had convinced her. It had taken some time, but she had eventually given in. She had only been with both of them a few times. As time passed, she had fallen out of love with Manoj. Her body still wanted his, so she had kept up their alliance, not out of love, but for the thrill of it, and because of the threat of Pankaj leaking a video he had secretly made of them.

Falguni had never had anyone to talk to about any of this. She could not confide in her girlfriends in Daltonganj; they were all judgemental prudes with their own secret lives. Falguni couldn't possibly have talked to Garima, seeing as she was her husband's sister. And anyway, Garima had never been with a man. The most she had done was kiss one of her girlfriends out of curiosity.

After the sex between Falguni and Gautam slowed down to a snail's pace, something magical happened. Falguni got pregnant.

'Natasha! Are you serious!' Gautam exclaimed.

Falguni had never seen Gautam this excited. Or excited at all.

'I think so. I got this test from CVS ...' Falguni offered it to him.

Gautam located the box it came in, read the instructions, asked Falguni some questions about the specifics of her urination method, and concluded that the test was in fact conducted in the prescribed manner. Just to be sure, they took a second test.

'I can't believe it. This is amazing news!' Gautam announced in the end. He held her by her shoulders, peered into her eyes and said earnestly, 'Natasha, you've given me so much happiness. I'll call home.'

What followed were the three most exciting months of Falguni's life. The prospect of this baby had finally fully erased her past life. She felt like a new person. She felt like Natasha.

She no longer needed secret, dirty affairs for a thrill. Or for her husband to choke her in bed. For the first time in her life, she didn't need cheap thrills and distractions from reality to sustain her. Because, for the first time in her life, she was genuinely happy.

Gautam was gentle with her. Every move he made showed how much he cared. Falguni had fallen in love with his tenderness, with him. For the first time in her life, she felt safe.

When she miscarried, their world shattered around them. Even though it was her body that suffered, her blood that soaked the rug, Gautam seemed to take it harder than her. It took them months to return to normal, to look each other in the eye. Falguni wanted to try again, reclaim everything she'd lost, but Gautam treated her like a porcelain doll – delicate, breakable.

He still loved her, she knew he did, but she missed his attention. He was too scared to try again. He didn't let himself hope. Falguni resented this. He was her whole world. She had had a taste of the full force of his love and attention on her, and she needed it back.

Desperate, she had to resort to lying about pain in her abdomen. She was on her period, but it was easy enough to pretend that it wasn't her time of the month, that the blood was inexplicable. She took off her underwear and stood in the bathroom for fifteen minutes, until a puddle of blood collected on the floor between her legs. Then, she stepped in it, and spread the blood on the floor to create a bigger, bloodier mess before screaming Gautam's name.

Terrified that it had something to do with the miscarriage, Gautam rushed her to the doctor. He was by her side, at her beck and call, whenever she needed him. He took time off from work. She was his priority again. When the doctors found nothing, and all the tests came back clean, she could only continue complaining of pain for so long before she had to put the matter to rest.

She needed something real. Or, if not, something that couldn't be dismissed by medical scans. That's when she invented chronic pain in her right arm. She groaned and moaned all day long. A general physician gave her muscle relaxants and eventually sent her to a physiotherapist. After months of therapy, she made no progress. The physiotherapist was baffled. He assigned her new exercises every week, monitored her range of movements closely, even changed her entire routine every other week, but there was no progress.

It was when she was prescribed pain medication that things really took a turn. She didn't take them at first, because she didn't need them, because the pain was a mere fragment of her imagination. But one day, boredom and the feeling of emptiness engulfed her more than usual, and she took one. That's when the addiction began.

This particular morning, she had called Gautam out of desperation. Her medication sometimes gave her a calming clarity. At other times, however, it made her feel helpless and paranoid. Today, it was the latter. Gautam had calmed her down, told her that she should rest, and he would try to come home from work early.

She had felt better, until she didn't. She called him again. He didn't pick up, and she spun out of control. By the time she called him the third time, she was desperate for attention, and could not think of a plan fast enough to secure it. So, without much thought, she made up an accident to get him to drop everything and come to her.

Now, he will be here any moment and Falguni still didn't have a plan. She had to make it look real. She had told him there was blood. Had she specified where the blood was coming from? Didn't she say she was chopping tomatoes with her bad arm? Had she said that she slipped and cut herself?

She needed to cut herself.

Falguni sprung to her feet. She pulled out the chopping board from the cupboard, three tomatoes from the fridge and placed them on the kitchen counter. She chopped the tomatoes, barely seeing anything she was doing, her eyes blurry with tears. With shaky fingers, she chopped as fast as she could.

How had it come to this? What had she done? If Gautam came home and saw that she had been lying to him, she would lose him. He would never trust her again. He wouldn't love her anymore. And she couldn't let that happen. He was her whole life now, her only life.

Maybe there was a way this could work … Maybe she could tell him everything. About Manoj and Pankaj forcing her, her father and brother beating her. Maybe he would give her a second chance. Maybe he could help her find something to do with her time. Maybe she could study further, even have a career. She could speak English quite fluently now, after all. Maybe there was a future for her beyond seeking Gautam's attention.

Just when she felt a glimmer of hope, she heard ambulance sirens. Were they coming for her? Had Gautam called 911?

'Fuck, fuck, fuck,' Falguni muttered to herself. Of course, Gautam would've called the ambulance! Why did she have to hang up on him and turn her phone off for the extra drama? He would've come home to her even without that part of the ruse. She cursed herself.

Falguni stumbled to the couch and picked up her phone. She held down the power button and waited for the screen to light up. What was she doing? Should she call him now? What would she say? If he had called the ambulance, it was too late now.

The sirens grew louder. Falguni stood rooted to the spot. If she didn't open the door, didn't say anything at all, would they break open the door?

'Fuck, fuck, fuck.'

She had pushed herself into a corner here. She knew what she had to do. Her chest rose and fell as she tried and failed to calm herself. She went back to the kitchen counter. With hands that shook violently, she picked up the knife again. How deep would the cut need to be to warrant the panicked phone call, begging her husband to come home? She'd told him that there was *so much blood, everywhere.* Would she need to chop a whole finger off? Would doctors be able to sew it back? Or would she spend the rest of her life without that finger?

'Fuck, fuck, fuck.'

🌹

Gautam didn't see an ambulance anywhere near the building when he got there. Had they already taken her away? He checked his watch, frantically racing up the stairs. It had taken him longer than usual; he shouldn't have taken a cab. He should've just run back home, as fast as he could.

When he got to the fourth floor, he ran to their apartment door. He paused for a moment, gathering himself, preparing for the worst. He slid his key into the lock and turned it open. When he pushed the door open and looked inside, he saw the last thing he had expected to see.

'Natasha …' he breathed.

Natasha sat there, on the couch, facing the door. When she saw him, she stood up, staring at him with wide eyes. She looked … fine. His eyes darted to the kitchen counter. Chopped tomatoes and no blood. He looked around. Nothing was out of place. His eyebrows came together in confusion.

'I'm sorry!' Natasha cried. 'I sent the ambulance away. I told them it was a prank. That I didn't know my husband would call them. They'll send us a bill.'

'I ... I don't ...' Gautam stammered. 'What's going on ...?'

She ran to him, looked at him with shiny, desperate eyes. 'I'm so sorry. I'll tell you everything. Please just ... listen to me. There's so much. I'm so trapped. My only other option was hurting myself. I can't do that to you again. I have to tell you the truth. Please, just hear me out.'

Natasha's voice sounded different. The expression on her face made her look like a completely different person. For the first time since their marriage, his wife looked ... scared of him. What was she so afraid of? Whatever it was, it couldn't be worse than the horrifying scenarios Gautam had been imagining for the last half hour. He shut the door behind him and walked inside.

'It's okay,' he said to her. Whatever it was, at least she was safe, and that mattered more to him than anything else. 'You can tell me anything.'

Talking to Strangers

The light pouring in through the tiny airplane window was blinding. Raveena squinted, as she angrily pulled out the buckle of her seat belt from under her. She caught the fingerhold on the flimsy window shade and slammed it shut. Now that she wasn't being attacked by sunlight and poked by a belt buckle, you'd expect that she would feel better. But no. Those were the least of her problems.

She was operating on three hours of sleep, zero caffeine and a debilitating migraine. To top that, she was in the middle of a mild nervous breakdown. She was careful not to complain about that to Shreya – her co-worker and partner on this business trip, who she had left behind. Shreya considered herself a staunch advocate of mental health. However, ironically, if you were to admit that you were struggling to cope, she would be the first one to tell you to stop exaggerating and taking attention away from those *really* suffering. She was essentially a self-appointed gatekeeper of mental health. Which is why, when Raveena had woken up in cold sweat in the middle of the night and decided to return home the next morning, she had done it quietly, without waking Shreya, who snored softly in the queen bed next to hers.

They still had three weeks left on their business trip, so they had to share the hotel room for that entire time. Raveena didn't dislike Shreya, but sharing a space for that long with any person can be challenging, especially if you already had so many other, larger problems to deal with.

Raveena leaned forward and rested her forehead against the seat in front of her. It was probably filthy, and her sensitive skin was likely to break out into pimples from it, but Raveena didn't have the bandwidth to care. She was already hurting, mentally and physically. What are a few pimples? A minuscule drop in the vast ocean of her gloom.

Raveena wondered if she was, in fact, exaggerating. It was possible. In Shreya's defence, she did read a lot about mental health on Instagram; maybe she knew what she was talking about. If Raveena could just get a handle on her migraine, she could sit back, line up all her other problems and arrange them in order of priority and gravity – worry about them in an organized manner. In their current jumbled state, she couldn't find the head or tail of anything.

And yet, there was more disappointment to be faced: she had forgotten to pack her medicine. She had taken a tablet the night before, and, as she slumped back in her seat now, she could visualize exactly where she had left the bottle on the bedside table. Upon summoning the flight attendant, Raveena was exasperated to find that the flight couldn't provide any pain medication to passengers. The flight attendant suggested Raveena purchase alcohol instead.

Raveena stared at the flight attendant's painted face, her own face clearly communicating: are you serious?

'I know it helps me,' the flight attendant joked uncomfortably. 'A drink or two when I'm feeling low.'

Raveena knew she should just smile and put the poor girl at ease, but the pettiness in her didn't let her perform this simple, small act of kindness. She remained silent.

'Anyway … we can't give out medication. It's against our policy.'

'Cool, thanks,' Raveena said dismissively.

'I'm sorry.'

As soon as the flight attendant walked away, face flushed, Raveena felt terrible about the way she had behaved. It wasn't the flight attendant's fault that she had forgotten her medicine, or that the airline had rules that the cabin crew was required to obey.

Not to mention, now that wine had been mentioned in their conversation, Raveena became aware of the fact that her throat was parched. And maybe alcohol would in fact help with the pain … But it was too late; the flight attendant was long gone, and Raveena had behaved too poorly to ask her to come back. Raveena settled in her seat, breathing deliberately, holding back tears of frustration and the resentment she felt towards herself. Sometimes, just sometimes, life could be so much easier if she just did what her brain was telling her to do. Instead, she had to go on and act like a rude brat, fully aware of what she was doing. Why couldn't she just handle her emotions? The education system had seriously failed in providing kids tools to handle themselves and their emotions at a later stage in life. And yet, they were forced to learn trigonometry, which a majority of them didn't require to use in everyday situations, for years. That was a fight for another day.

Raveena picked up her handbag from the seat next to her and dug out her water bottle. She took a long, desperate swig of water, looking at the bright side: no one was sitting next to her, which meant no battles for elbow room, at least for the first leg of the flight. Small mercies, she said to herself. When the same flight attendant came by to ask passengers to pull up their window shades for take-off, Raveena did so without any resistance. She let the sunglasses perched on top of her head drop on the bridge of her nose and rested her head back, eyes closed, lips parted, breath rapid.

Once they were airborne, Raveena waited for the flight attendant to come around, apologized for her rudeness and felt even more terrible than before when the flight attendant responded cheerfully, 'It's okay. We've all had headaches. I hope you feel better soon.'

Raveena's lips stretched in a tight smile. Why couldn't the flight attendant have been rude to her in return? Why couldn't she have been one of those vapid girls who spoke in English to passengers who clearly couldn't comprehend a word of it, and the more they didn't understand, the more the flight attendant insisted on speaking in English, and continued repeating the same words with different emphasis and increasing hostility, over and over again until everyone around them was uncomfortable and the poor, embarrassed passenger said they didn't want anything from the cart?

It's much easier to be rude to those types of people. 'Thank you,' Raveena said instead. 'I'm having a really bad day and I shouldn't have taken it out on you.'

'It's really okay,' the flight attendant said good-naturedly. She then went on with her job of handing out wasteful little plastic water bottles.

Raveena restrained herself from blurting out, 'I'm breaking up with my boyfriend of eight years. He's my whole life, but now I need a whole new life. We love each other, but we're no longer *in* love with each other. Nothing's wrong with our relationship; it's simply run its course. There's no point dragging it out till it slowly dies. We're unappreciative and unromantic. We took something extraordinary and made it ordinary through years of neglect and gradual decay. And we didn't see it, till I came here, to a new city, worked in a new office, met new people, and realized that there is a new life to be lived outside of the only life I had ever lived, the only future I had imagined. So, I'm going home to leave my boyfriend. To free us to pursue new avenues, build new futures. It's the right thing to do: to give us both clean slates.'

Long after the flight attendant had left, behind the slim curtains at the back of the cabin, long after everyone had drained the palmful of water and crumpled up the plastic bottles that would most likely end up in landfills, if not in the ocean, and shoved them into the back pockets of the seats in front of them, Raveena thought about how if her company hadn't sent her on this eight-week business trip and opened her eyes to a new world, she would never have had the courage to end her relationship and her old life, and start afresh.

🌹

Miraculously, the thunderous screech of rubber on tarmac didn't cause Raveena to stir. She had consumed two small plastic glasses of quite terrible red wine and obsessed over every thought that crowded her conscious mind till she had fallen asleep. Then, in her dreams, she obsessed over more thoughts, the ones that crowded her unconscious mind. She was only awakened when an older man in a brown cardigan asked her to remove her handbag from what was to be his seat in the second leg of her journey.

As soon as Raveena lifted her head, she had an overwhelming feeling that she was floating ... or drowning. Contrary to the flight attendant's belief, wine actually does the opposite of how painkillers work.

The older man was looking at her with concern and confusion. 'Are you okay?' he asked gently, as if trying to be as non-intrusive as possible.

'Head hurts,' Raveena mumbled, the small-town Indian girl in her feeling ashamed for having consumed alcohol and now suffering the consequences in front of an adult. She had to remind herself that she was twenty-nine years old and owed no explanations to this stranger.

'Ah, do you need a painkiller? I have a wide variety.'

'Yes, please,' Raveena blurted out, immediately forgetting her shame from a moment ago. He could most likely smell the alcohol on her, as he sat next to her, but there was no judgement in his expression as he ruffled through his cloth tote bag and unearthed a raggedy pouch with a broken zipper.

'Thank you, uncle,' Raveena said, taking the strip of tablets from him. She wondered briefly if she would've accepted tablets from a stranger if they were in an unsealed bottle, and, at this point, in this much pain, she probably would have, against her better judgement. Thankfully, these tablets were in a strip, wrapped individually, in what looked like on-brand packaging. One less thing to worry about. Raveena waited for the tablets to dissolve in the remaining water in her bottle, before gulping it down greedily.

By the time the plane took off, Raveena's head had stopped throbbing. She felt like a different person, as though the pile of bricks that she had been carrying on her head had been removed and she could lift her head again. She looked towards her neighbour with a grateful smile.

'You saved my life,' she said. Maybe she did tend to exaggerate.

'No problem, beta,' her neighbour said. 'Where are you going?'

Kind of a redundant question, Raveena thought, since their flight had one destination, then kicked herself for being a smartass. He was just trying to make conversation. 'Home,' she said instead.

'I'm going to visit my son,' he offered.

'Oh, that's nice.'

'He's having a baby. My first grandchild.' The pride and affection in his voice triggered something in Raveena. Suddenly, she was under water again.

'Congratulations,' she said, blinking rapidly to force away the tears that flooded her eyes. She failed.

'Oh ... what happened?' the older man asked, looking panic-stricken to find a woman half his age crying out of the blue. 'Was it something I said?'

'No, I'm sorry. I'm sorry. You didn't say anything. I'm just ... a mess.' It took her several moments to compose herself.

The man looked pained, and absolutely lost. He had most likely only wanted to kill time with some polite small talk, not dive deep into her emotional crisis. But in that moment, Raveena couldn't hold anything in. She had fully lost control of her emotions. Every day, every hour was a struggle. She would be fine one minute and the next minute, without warning, spin out of control. Despite what Shreya would have to say about her situation, Raveena had privately searched Google for answers. The results indicated that she was in the midst of a mental breakdown, but she was too scared to say those words out loud, in fear of trivializing something so significant ... when her problems seemed so insignificant.

Nothing had even happened. She had moved temporarily to a new city for a project and, for the first time in her life, imagined a different future for herself. Nothing was even wrong with her old projected future. She had simply become obsessed with the idea of a new life, and now was on her way to pull the trigger to end her old life. That's all. It hardly warranted a full-blown breakdown. Perhaps Shreya was right; Raveena was probably exaggerating.

'I'm leaving my boyfriend,' she cried. 'It has to end. We've run our course. It's time to move on.'

She spoke more to herself than to him. He nodded quietly.

'I don't even know why we're together anymore. We just … are. We fell in love, got into a relationship … and just stayed. Never questioned it. But there's so much more out there. There's newness … excitement, romance, possibilities.' Raveena paused, then added thoughtfully, 'There's also rejection, loneliness and … despair, I guess. But I'd rather try, than just stagnate because I'm too scared to be alone. Or scared that I'd miss him. What kind of a sad stereotype am I?'

She turned to him, seeking answers he clearly wasn't in the place to provide. When he didn't say anything, she asked, 'What should I do?'

'I thought the decision was made?' he said.

'Yes … I mean, yes, I know it's the right thing to do. But now I'm thinking about him. For him, it'll come out of nowhere. I don't know how he would take it. And he didn't do anything wrong … So it's not like he deserves to be dumped.' Imagining his face made her weak with emotion, but, in the next moment, she hardened. 'Or maybe he wouldn't even really notice my absence from his life. He'll just go on living … There's no passion left in our relationship. I can't just assume that he'd be heartbroken if I left.'

Her words hung in the space between them. When he still didn't speak after a few minutes, Raveena asked, 'Do you have any advice? Anything to help me in the right direction?'

'I can't make the decision for you. I don't know you. I don't know your boyfriend. But I do know relationships ...' he trailed off. He closed his eyes for a moment, and Raveena waited patiently. She had never ever said the words she had said to this man out loud. She needed to hear thoughts that didn't come from her own head.

He opened his eyes and said, 'I don't have experience with ... shopping, when it comes to relationships. I was married young, and the only woman I have ever known is my wife. We got married thirty-five years ago. I really am no expert in searching for the right partner. I only know how to be a life partner to my wife. And while passion and excitement are wonderful in a partnership, I've found that for sustenance, we also need companionship, trust and affection. I always think of marriage or family ... as a plant. Passion and romance are flowers. They are seasonal; they bloom every once in a while, brighten everything up. But as lovely as they are, the plant needs healthy roots to survive. Our marriage is rooted in love, trust and respect. Over the years, we've developed branches with laughter, conversation, experiences, having children, and now ... our first grandchild.'

Raveena was overwhelmed. As profound and valuable as his words were, she couldn't find a way to apply them to her own life. Thirty-five years ago, his parents found a stranger for him to marry, and he made it work. Her situation was hardly comparable. Things have changed. You no longer have to be with someone just because you're expected to, and somehow find a way to make it work. She didn't have to settle.

'One last thing about this plant analogy: you have to water it. And that's the work. If you don't water it, it could have everything else it needs, but still wither away. You can't expect a plant to survive without water, let alone bloom.'

'But *is* your plant still blooming? Or just surviving? Are you still in love?'

'Very much so. Maybe not the kind of love your generation needs.' His tone, miraculously, still lacked judgement, despite Raveena's obvious scepticism. He chuckled and added, 'But I know you probably don't have the same views on love. So, here's a quirky little question you can ask yourself about your partner.' He paused for impact, before asking, 'How would you feel if he was gravely ill? Or if he died?'

'What?' Raveena was shaken. 'That's dark and dramatic!'

The old man chuckled. 'Maybe. But it works. I only thought of it when my wife had to be hospitalized, seven years ago. We almost lost her, and that fear of losing her made me love her even deeper. So, if you think about your partner dying, on a scale of devastation to relief, where would you land?'

'I'm so sorry your wife got sick. And glad she recovered. But this is no way to make life decisions, by being ruled by emotions. This is really extreme and crazy!' Raveena said, still in disbelief. She couldn't even bear to think about Atul dying. Her brain refused to imagine that scenario.

'Well then, make it less extreme: how would you feel if they were with someone else? Happy and fulfilled.'

Of all the things he had said to her in the past few minutes – arguably deeper and much better thought-out things – this hit Raveena the hardest. All the time she had spent mulling over their upcoming break-up, she had been thinking about her life, her future. Now, when she thought about leaving Atul, and him actually moving on … with someone else … her heart couldn't contain it. She wouldn't be able to call him anymore. Someone else would kiss him. He would never try to make her laugh again, delivering a silly joke and waiting eagerly for her to crack up. She could never hold on to him during heart-wrenching episodes of *Grey's Anatomy*. He would comfort someone else.

Her heart raced, and, in that vulnerable moment, her mind went back to the first question: what if Atul died? He would be gone, she couldn't call him, hear his voice, feel his warmth, the touch of his lips, she couldn't tell him about her day and listen to him talk about his. They couldn't buy a house together, make it a home, sleep in the same bed, next to each other, every night for the rest of their lives. She was breathing heavily.

The older man said something, but it didn't register. Her mind went back to the plant analogy. Maybe their relationship didn't have flowers anymore. That's it. That's all that was missing: some fun, some romance. But that was hardly a surprise. When was the last time either of them had tried to do something special for each other? When was the last time they watered their plant? Also, just because they didn't have any flowers now, didn't mean that their relationship would not bloom again. And how easily had she put all the blame for the lack of flowers on Atul and decided to rip the entire plant from its root, discard it?

Her ears were ringing. What was she doing? What was wrong with her? She loved him, and he loved her; so why was she running away from the work that a relationship required and trying to replace him with a new city?

The older man was softly patting her on her back.

'There's something wrong with me,' Raveena whispered. 'Something is broken. I don't know what. And instead of dealing with it, I'm blaming everything on him.' Atul was the one person who had always loved her, but whatever was going on in her mind made her fascinated with the idea of completely erasing her old life and starting over. As though just like that, she could leave all her problems behind and become a new person. When, in reality, all she wanted was for him to move to the city with her. She couldn't live in that town anymore. The walls were closing in on her, and she needed to escape, with him by her side. The truth was that she was too afraid to ask him so instead she had convinced herself that she didn't need him. That he didn't fit in her future plans. This way, she could reject him before he could reject her, and it would be less painful, because she would be prepared, in control.

Now that she had laid out all her thoughts in a recognizable, readable order, her plan to leave Atul looked stupid. She was stunned at the thought of what she had almost done.

When the plane landed shortly after, Raveena, still shaken and emotional, said goodbye to the older man. 'Congratulations on your grandbaby,' she added as they waited for their bags. 'When is your wife going to meet the baby?'

'Oh,' the older man said, looking away, at the baggage belt. 'She's already here. She came early, for the delivery.'

Raveena smiled. 'Well, I hope you have a great time with your family. Or, should I say, your well-tended plant?'

Just then, Raveena spotted Atul waiting for her at the gate. Her heart melted. She couldn't wait for her bag to arrive, so she could run to him and hold him. The conversation with the stranger on the plane had played a large part in changing her mind, but seeing Atul now, she knew that she wouldn't have been able to go through with her silly plan regardless. She loved him too much.

Enough to tell him the truth. To ask for help. Something was wrong; her mental breakdowns were rooted in a cause. And now that she stopped placing the blame on Atul, she could see clearly that something needed to change. Raveena was comforted by Atul's smiling face. She wasn't going to be alone in this.

🌹

Prakash shuffled to the gate, dragging his suitcase behind him. He spotted his son rushing towards him. Prakash waved, wiping his cheeks. He had to purse his lips together, as he watched the young woman from the plane embrace her partner.

He hadn't had the heart to tell her that his wife's sickness had taken her seven years ago. But he was glad that he hadn't needed to break her heart like that; that a hypothetical scenario had been enough to show her the light. Whatever it was that she and her partner were dealing with could be solved. They had youth and health on their side. They would figure the rest out.

Prakash looked towards his son, beaming at him as he approached. His daughter-in-law was waving at him through a rolled-down car window. Prakash gulped. The plant of his family had suffered a drought when his wife had passed away. But, any day now, they were going to welcome a new branch, and flowers would bloom again.

Circle

How was his wife, even at nine months pregnant, ready to give birth any moment now, still stronger than him? It didn't make any sense. Aakash wished for some of that strength, keeping both his hands firmly on the wheel. His eyes stayed on the road, but his ears were tuned in to every breath Mansi took. He was watching for change. Knowing Mansi, she would play down her discomfort, so he took on the responsibility of looking out for her. If her breath became shorter by even a fraction, or a moan escaped her lips, he would turn the car towards the hospital. Aakash looked in the rear-view mirror to ensure, for the tenth time, that they had the hospital bag packed and ready in the back seat.

'Aakash, can you relax? You're starting to freak me out,' Mansi groaned from the passenger seat.

'I *am* relaxed,' he said quietly. His wife didn't actually need a response from him. She could read him like an open book.

'Really? Because it looks like you're choking that steering wheel. And you won't look at me!'

Aakash glanced towards her shortly before returning his gaze to the road. 'I'm driving,' he said shortly, evenly.

'Can you at least put one hand on the gear, so I can hold it? The baby needs it.'

Knowing fully well that she was using the baby growing inside her to get her way, Aakash followed her instructions. Mansi placed her right hand on top of his left and squeezed it. Despite himself, he felt better.

'Do you want to talk about it?' she prodded.

'There's nothing to—'

'*Do you want to talk about it?*' Mansi asked again, this time, her tone making it clear that refusing wasn't an option.

It took a moment for Aakash to form the words. What he was feeling was very simple, very obvious, but still, somehow, saying it out loud, putting words to his fear, left his body cold. 'What if he says no?'

Mansi's grip on his hand grew stronger. She didn't respond, not knowing what to say.

Aakash hated how small his voice sounded, like he was seventeen again. Like it was the day after his mother died, finally succumbing to her illness, after struggling for seven long months. They had seen it coming, the doctors had 'prepared' them; however, when it happened, it still wasn't any less of a shock.

Intellectually, his brain understood what had happened, but emotionally, he couldn't absorb it. Even his body reacted in a completely foreign way, convulsing and aching like it had never done before. The grief choked his insides, from the back of his throat all the way down to his gut. He wasn't prepared for it. Some nights it felt downright violent, like a limb had been ripped off his body. It felt cruel and unnecessary.

And then, after he had got somewhat used to the loss of his mother, his eyes landed on his father. Somehow, that cut even deeper. The look on his father's face knocked the breath out of Aakash. Before that, he had never seen his father quite so … crumpled. Even when they'd found out about his mother's illness, even through the diagnostic tests, the surgeries, the recoveries, stints in the hospital, uncertainty, even through her health declining slowly, till she reached her end – his father had appeared strong. He had cried, he had held her hands and revisited the good memories they had shared, he had broken down when she was in the operation theatre, but this … This was different.

After she was gone, his father had finally allowed himself to break.

For the seven months of his mother's final fight, no matter how much of a toll it had taken on their mental and physical health, they had been able to keep going – because they had had something to focus on. Once that was gone, once the funeral was over and everyone had returned to their lives, that's when the loss settled in. That's when they looked ahead at the rest of their lives, at how empty it was going to be without her.

At first, Aakash and his father were gentle with each other. They spoke quietly at the dinner table, they took turns looking at each other and they didn't talk about her. They didn't ask each other how they were doing, and they didn't share their own sadness, not in words. Slowly, they turned on the TV at dinner time, the hum of reality TV, singing and dancing shows, drowning out the need for conversation.

Their first argument was when his father found out that Aakash hadn't applied to colleges in the city, and instead, planned to stay on in their small-town home. His father had seemed more sad than angry at his son's decision. He could see why Aakash had decided to stay, in their small town, where opportunities for him were quite limited, and that guilt ate away at him. He wanted the best for Aakash. He couldn't bear to see his son curb his dreams this way; not for him.

Aakash refused to listen to anything his father had to say. He knew that despite what he was acknowledging, his father needed him there, and he needed his father. They had lost their glue, and, if Aakash didn't actively make decisions to stay together, he feared that they might drift apart. He had to find a way to stay together, to not lose his father too.

There was love between them, of course there was. The father–son bond was powerful. However, neither of them was outspoken or very good with words. It was after his mother was gone that Aakash realized her significant role in bringing light and laughter to their family. Without her, everything lost its shine, became dreary.

So, Aakash had stayed. In the end, he was sure his father had secretly been relieved, even happy with his decision. Aakash had gone to college in their town. He had met Mansi. They had become close friends during the four years of college, but never dated. Mansi had big dreams for her life, and Aakash didn't want to get in her way. They spent all their time together, studying, laughing, listening to music, just being there for each other.

When they graduated four years later, Mansi had a job waiting for her in the city. Aakash took a job in his town. Each doing what they needed to do. It broke their hearts. They parted with promises of keeping in touch.

It was only after one year of distance that they came closer in a different, deeper way than the four years of seeing each other every day. So, Aakash found a job in her city and asked her to marry him. She was his future. He couldn't let her slip away.

They got married in their town. If his father felt any sadness at all about Aakash's impending departure, he didn't show it. Not once. That stung Aakash. How could his father not care? For the first time in his life, he wouldn't live under the same roof as his father. And after facing a loss of this magnitude, after grieving together for so long, didn't his departure affect his father at all? It hurt even more because Aakash was breaking inside. His decision made him extremely vulnerable.

After staying home with his father for five years after his mother's death, Aakash finally left. It was at the airport that he felt his father's body tremble when they hugged goodbye. Aakash held him tighter. Every fibre in his body wanted to stay. The thought of his father waking up to an empty house, making breakfast alone, watching TV alone ... broke Aakash's heart. It took every ounce of strength he had to let go. He couldn't have done it without Mansi by his side.

'Do you promise you'll visit us in a month? For Holi?' she asked his father.

'I promise,' he said, his smile releasing the tears that had built up in his eyes. He treated Mansi like the daughter he'd never had. And, due to that closeness, he could speak to her freely, without embarrassment, in a way he could never speak to Aakash. They were both too awkward.

'Okay, good,' she chirped. Her tone was light, but Aakash knew her well enough to sense the emotions she was hiding. 'And the month after that, we'll come home for your birthday.'

For two years, they had done exactly that, visiting each other often, sharing their lives through phone calls. That no longer felt enough.

'I don't think he will,' Mansi said now.

'He has never said yes! I've asked him to move here with us so many times! He just won't do it. Won't leave that house ...' Aakash's fingers were cold. Every time they'd said goodbye in the past two years, it had gotten harder. How manymore of these visits did they have left? 'He's not doing well, especially since Goyal Uncle died. He has no one to talk to, and he's retired. There's nothing left for him in that town. But he won't budge. You don't know how stubborn he is ...'

His voice trailed off. There he was, his father, standing outside Gate 4, next to his suitcase. He was wearing the backpack Aakash had bought him, and the size of it made him look frailer. Aakash's jaw hardened. 'There's no way

I'm letting him say no this time. He needs us; he needs his family.'

'Exactly, we'll convince him. Don't worry,' Mansi said. 'And now that I have a secret weapon ...'

Aakash glanced at her and followed her gaze to her very large bump. He couldn't help but smile. 'You're going to use your pregnancy to emotionally blackmail him?'

'Of course! For now. And, after the delivery, the cuteness of our baby, his grandchild, will do the rest. Done deal!' Mansi looked pleased with herself.

Aakash felt lighter, more confident about the outcome of their proposal. He parked the car and turned to kiss Mansi's forehead. 'Be right back,' he murmured. He rubbed her belly before rushing out.

Aakash took confident strides towards his father. He waved, feeling a thrill rush through him. His father waved back, raising himself on the tips of his toes to make himself bigger, more visible. Just looking at his father's demeanour, the emotion on his face – expectant, wistful, tender – Aakash felt as though the battle had been won. The man looked like a grandfather, and he needed to be with his grandchild.

Hi, everyone! Inspired by all the different, heart-warming stories we've been seeing circulate the online space, I decided to document a day in my life, my experience sharing a space with my partner, Adil. I'm excited to share the story with you. Hope it resonates with you. Let me know what you think in the comments down below. Happy reading!

Self-care Day

This had been a great idea, to take a self-care day to reset and recalibrate. Leena had been confined with Adil for over a month, sheltering from a global pandemic, and, by this point, they were at each other's throats. They had begun bickering about irrelevant things and, lately, they had been finding themselves midway through arguments, unable to remember what they were even fighting about.

Their small, one-bedroom flat in Mulund West, in suburban Mumbai, made it nearly impossible for them to have any personal space. But after watching her favourite YouTuber's latest video about self-care, Leena had decided that the only way to get things back on track in their relationship was to take time away from each other. Adil had looked hurt when she'd suggested it the previous night, but she had insisted, and he had agreed in the end. The first step was successfully accomplished: *schedule your self-care time, and guard it with passion*.

While Adil valiantly gave up the desk by the window in the living room for her and hunched over his laptop perched on a breakfast tray in the window-less bedroom, Leena focused on hitting everything on her list. So far, her day had been perfect. She'd used the extra time to do her hair in the morning, decluttered her desk, and been more mindful and present all day, as prescribed. She had even gone up to the terrace for a walk during her lunch break, using her scarf as a mask, just in case she passed someone on the staircase.

Once her last virtual meeting for the day had ended, Leena unrolled her yoga mat, ready for a thirty-minute practice, followed by a cold shower.

She'd barely started her warm-ups when Adil poked his head out of their bedroom. 'Can I come out, or will I be disturbing you?' he asked.

'I finished work, so you won't be disturbing me,' Leena said, keeping her tone neutral. It was important to put up a wall and discourage conversation, so she could really be alone with her *self*.

'Can I use the kitchen?'

Leena broke character. 'Yes! Come on, Adil, don't act like I'm some kind of evil dictator and you need to ask permission to eat!'

'Just asking …' Adil said, not looking at her as he walked to the kitchen, muttering under his breath. 'I can't keep up with all the new rules you make …'

Leena ignored that. He was usually the sensible one in the couple and she the volatile troublemaker, so this behaviour was unlike him. But she put Adil out of her thoughts, plugged in her headphones and followed along with the yoga video. As her shoulders stretched and relaxed, she reclaimed her zen.

However, that didn't last long. Soon the aroma of spices wafted from the kitchen, and her stomach grumbled. What was Adil cooking? Was he making enough for both? *Stop*. She pushed the thought of food away and sank deeper into her *utkatasana*. That's it. That felt good. She just needed to focus. However, as she took a deep breath, the unmistakable smell of MTR's pav bhaji masala filled her nostrils.

'Ugh, forget it,' she muttered. Leena stood up, rolled her mat and marched to the bathroom. Better. The torturous smell of bhaji couldn't reach here. And once again she felt calmer as she turned on the shower and the cold water prickled her back. The smell of her soap overpowered every other thought, but not the grumbling of her stomach. He was doing this on purpose; he knew full well that she had a weakness for pav bhaji.

She took her time in the shower, refusing to give in to Adil's twisted trap. However, despite all her efforts, minutes later, she found herself watching Adil eat at the counter, as her hair dripped water on the tiled kitchen floor. Leena scanned the kitchen, her heart sinking.

'You really didn't make me any?' Her voice broke.

Adil took a moment to finish chewing. He looked up at her just as, to her embarrassment, tears had started to fill her eyes. He nodded towards the living room.

Leena walked over to find her dinner waiting for her at her desk, where she'd had her lunch, alone, away from her loving husband, who was always considerate and generous, and put up with her quirks and erratic nature. As much as she'd needed her self-care time, suddenly she felt a terrible longing for Adil.

She picked up her plate, walked back to the kitchen, and pulled up a stool next to him at the counter. He looked at her, but didn't speak. As they ate quietly, Leena let the pav bhaji blissfully overwhelm all her senses while she thought of ways to get back on his good side.

So ... that didn't go exactly as planned. But you know what? I don't regret trying, and I also don't regret what the experience taught me. Do I have a tendency to overthink? Yes. Do I create bigger problems out of small problems? Maybe.

The truth is that we feel this need to fix every problem we have. Anytime anything makes us unhappy, we try to change it. When we fail at making ourselves feel better, we feel even worse. Why do we take on this responsibility of feeling happy when we're feeling sad? Sometimes, we just have to live with how we feel.

I read somewhere that all feelings are for feeling. That includes the bad and sad ones too. The pursuit of being happy all the time is a futile endeavour. Life is full of ups and downs. So, the next time I feel low, I'll let myself feel that way for a little while. And the next time I feel high, I'll cherish that moment and fly as high as I can.

ANYTHING

Your chin rested on the fist of your right hand as you leaned on the high table of the coffee shop, only half-sitting on the wooden stool, your feet flat on the floor. Your eyes met mine just as I entered and I immediately tried to convert my snicker at your moustache into a friendly smile. Your beard, just like your moustache, was sparse and light. You've always had trouble growing facial hair, haven't you? Your thick and dark hair, perched chaotically on your head, more than compensates for it. You don't need a beard or a moustache, but I didn't tell you that the first time we met. You got up, exposed your even, white teeth and gave me a big squeeze, like you were greeting an old friend, which immediately put me at ease. You engaged me in conversation almost instantly, surprising me with your openness and the sparkle in your eyes. You were a contrast to everyone else I knew in that unfamiliar city, where I had grown accustomed to tight lips and unfeeling eyes. Your coffee, topped with cream and sugar, placed next to mine, dark and bitter. You sat across from me, your eyes alive and merry, my chin rested on the fist of my right hand as I leaned on the high table of the coffee shop.

I pretend to be asleep as I hear you moving around the hospital room; the scent of your aftershave strong in my nostrils. I can smell it, even over the violent stench of sterility surrounding us, a stench I have come to associate with home. I haven't been home in days, ever since I puked blood. I know it ends here. I also know that I'm being too pessimistic – I know because you keep reminding me about it. I never, however, point out how excessively optimistic you are being, and how much that infuriates me. I want to shake it out of you, pull you into the deep ditch of despair with me. I feel a tingle of cool air, making me shiver as the door opens. I have half a mind to tolerate the cold, but before I can decide, you've already readjusted the blankets over me. I am cocooned inside a clean gown, lying on clean sheets and covered in layers of clean blankets. I have never felt this dirty, my rotten insides decaying further inside me. I hear you talking to the nurse, shrugging away the admiration she showers on you for being a good boyfriend. I hear your quiet laughter ringing in my ears, slipping down my throat like raw egg yolk. I gulp, but fail to eliminate the taste of metal from my tongue. I know it ends here.

You said you know that they were in a good place, Benjamin and Elaine. You read Benjamin's enigmatic expression, which Elaine adopts too, at the very end of the film as only a brief moment of panic. You were certain that it was going to pass, and they were going to find their happily ever after. You see, I don't believe in those. You stuffed your mouth with popcorn, as you happily talked about how they were meant to be, and how glad it made you feel that after their long and hard struggle, they eloped to be together. You didn't recognize their expressions at all, did you? You weren't familiar with the silent terror they felt in their bones, leaving them numb yet tortured. You couldn't see that it wasn't a beginning, but an end. You said it was your favourite film when I told you it was mine. You insisted that we watch it together. You sat under the feeble light of the glass lantern hanging from the ceiling, your eyebrows casting a shadow above your cheek. You leaned in towards me for a kiss, but I got up, pretending to not have noticed that gesture, asking you if you'd like some more wine. You offered to pour us both some more and pulled me back down on the couch. You shuffled around the kitchen, cheerfully talking about your theories on the ending of *The Graduate*, while I thought about how you said it was your favourite film when I told you it was mine.

I wipe my palms on the starchy hospital gown and feel more sweat appear rapidly. I am hot, and I am cold. I kick the sheets away and pull the ends of my fuzzy red cardigan closer to my chest. I feel the bed compress as you sit down next to me and snake your arm around my waist. I know you're being affectionate, like you always are, but I can't help myself from cringing away. I am not surprised that it doesn't dishearten you, and your hold only gets tighter. I concentrate on my breathing, counting deliberately as I suck in the dry air, hold it for just a beat and then release it. I barely register the words you whisper to me, only the reassuring tone in which you talk. I check the clock on the wall directly in front of me, counting down the minutes till when the doctor will be here with the test results. I suck in a long, uneven breath, the look on the nurse's face when she informed us that the results were here but the doctor will tell us more, branded in my brain. I, despite myself, feel your faith seep into my skin. I see it happen. I begin to hope, even as my heart beats louder than ever. I wipe my palms on the gown and reach for your hand.

You insisted that I come to the coffee shop after work that night, two summers later, which didn't make sense to me. You refused to see reason when I explained to you that I was tired and in need of a cold beer, not coffee. You didn't laugh at the messy bun that I had rolled my hair into, sitting atop my head. You had shaved off your moustache, which I noticed instantly, which you noticed me noticing, which brought a smile to our lips. You had somehow convinced the barista to keep the shop open for us. You had her bring our order, the same one we had had the first time we met, to the same table we had first sat at. You half-sat on a wooden stool with your feet flat on the floor, while my chin rested on the fist of my right hand as I leaned on the high table of the coffee shop. You took a sip from your cup and reached for my hand, and suddenly everyone important to us appeared from behind the counter and pillars, under the tables, everywhere. You held on to my hand as you dropped down on one knee, mistaking my shock for surprise. You spoke about the first time we met, and all the times after that, as familiar faces stared back at me, lips stretched into wide smiles, eyes glazed with tears.

I clutch your hand as we sit in tight embrace, the doctor in front of us – frigid and still. I'm unable to look away from his face, staring at him silently till he looks at you and asks if we're ready. I nod, ever so slightly, and hear you say yes. I hear the crack in your voice. I hear your heart pound in your chest. I can't stand it. I'm the pessimist, not you. I'm the one supposed to drag you down, and you're the one supposed to prop me up. I'm doing my part and you're bailing on yours, upsetting the balance of our entire relationship. I know what he's going to say even before he says it. I always knew it ends here. I don't need confirmation. I look away from his face to yours. I follow the teardrop that escapes the corner of your eye, and I collect it on my finger. I make measured movements, afraid that moving too much will make me die faster. I hear what he is saying in your face, in your sniffs and your gentle trembles. I see it in the way you don't look at me; I feel it in the way your fingers crush mine. I feel it in the dryness of my lips, the raggedness of my breath. I don't want to feel it anymore, when your body shakes and heaves as you pull me closer. I fall into your desperate embrace, frigid and still.

You said family is what's most important to you. You told me I was your family now and assured me that your relatives would love me, your new fiancée. You brought me to your home, promising to be by my side the entire time. You lied. You disappeared right after introducing me to your parents. You went up to your old room, excusing yourself for a second to take a phone call, leaving me glancing towards the dark stairwell, giggling nervously at your father's jokes. You told me they would love me, but I could tell that your mother didn't. You have her dark eyes, and your father's every other feature. Later, you sat next to me at the dinner table, and I kept my eyes lowered, out of anger and nerves. You laughed comfortably, contagiously, and soon we were all having the good time that you promised. You disappeared once again, at the end of dinner, leaving me alone with your parents a second time. But this time, the air felt warmer. You returned with your brightest smile, like your ploy had been successful. You hugged your parents goodbye and they hugged me goodbye and, once in the car, we hugged each other. You made me a part of your family that night.

I have told you so many times that I don't want to see anyone. I see the sadness in their eyes, but I see the pity too. I don't want to be pitied. I am resigned to my fate. I feel that part of my meagre time with you is being robbed from me when others are present. I search for you, my eyes darting from one mournful face to another. I am alive, but they look at me as though they're seeing my dead body. I smile weakly at my mother's face, and my father wraps his arm around her, bringing her to me. I feel my throat close up as they sit beside me on the bed and look up towards the door. I follow their gaze to find you and your parents. I see the red bridal *chunni*, embroidered in gold, that your mother is holding, and the little box of sindoor in your palm. I am not interested in this drama, but have decided to endure it. I didn't expect the flood of emotions that engulf me, surrounded by the people I love the most, grieving my death while I'm still alive. I begin to sob as our mothers fuss over me, making me pretty for my groom. I touch your face as you draw a straight line with vermilion through the parting in my hair. I do not deserve you. I never did anything to deserve someone as generous and affectionate as you. I don't want to ever leave you, but, if I have to, I can't imagine a better way to depart than dying in your arms.

You refuse to let go of me, long after I'm gone. You cling to my lifeless body. You weep into my chest. You're talking to me and I hear you, looking down at you. You tell me how you would give anything to get me back. You tell me that I was your reason to live. You talk to me about the kids we never had. You share with me the dreams that were never realized. You whisper into my heart about the beautiful nights that we spent together. You tell me how you regret the pain that I was in towards the end, how you would have happily traded your own health for my suffering. You lift yourself up, off my cold body and study my face. Your body shakes violently, your eyes the colour of faded blood. Your hair is patchy, your lips like chalk. You aren't speaking anymore. You look around the silent room in desperation, searching for … what? Your gaze rests on my closed eyelids, willing them to open for you, to take away your misery. You hold both my hands in yours and rest your elbows on the bed. You sniff back your tears. You look up, directly at me.

I watch you from above. I feel cool air blast from behind me, throwing my hair into my face. I turn around to a tall, dark figure staring down at me. I glide backwards, only to find myself trapped, without an escape in sight. I see the dark figure approach me, I see you on the other side. I can't come back to you. I don't know where to go. I wait. I watch.

                              I freeze when it comes closer to me.

        I have a choice, it tells me.

        I know I do. I had heard you say *anything* too.

                              I have a decision to make.

                I can go back, live.

                I can live, but you have to die.

          I can't live if you die, no.

                              I bargain for your life.

        I can live, if you lose your legs.

                                              I watch.

You will feel my faint heartbeat under your palm. You will jump up in shock, exhilaration. You will squeal, leap and sprint till someone hears you. You will inform them of the miracle. You will follow the doctor back to my room and watch her confirm your belief. You will hold me till the world pauses for us and time ceases to exist. You will plant your forehead against mine, as tears flow freely down our cheeks. You brought me back to life and you will nurse me back to health. You will feed me, you will bathe me, you will read to me. You will be at my service, day and night, yielding to even my smallest demands. You will hold my hand and shiver with euphoria when the doctors tell us that I will be fine. You will be buoyant, dear husband. You will be the happiest man on the planet. You will arrange for all my belongings to be brought over to your house – our new home. You will animatedly recount our blessings to our friends and family visiting us at the hospital. You will wipe the sweat off my forehead when I wake up in the middle of the night, haunted by a nightmare, a curse. You will take me to our new home. You will lose your legs.

I will see it happen. I will agree with you when you express disbelief that a fall that minor claimed both your legs. I will express my shock at your paralysis. I will drive you to the hospital for repeated tests, till they figure out what's causing your bones to freeze. I will roll your wheelchair to the doctor's desk. I will adjust the blanket over your lifeless legs and clutch your clammy hands. I will scream at the doctor and blame him for this tragedy. I will cause a scene and threaten to sue the hospital. I will do it, so you don't have to. I will do it for as long as you need me to. I will stop when you grow tired. I will take you to our new home. I will feed you, bathe you, read to you. I will be at your service, day and night, yielding to even your smallest demands. I will work from home, so that I can be with you whenever you need me. I will buy you the exorbitantly priced wheelchair we read about online. I will not tell you the truth behind my miracle and your catastrophe. I will know with every bone in my body that I couldn't live without you. I will stand by your side. I will make love to you when you lie awake at night. I will let you be powerful in the dark. I will let you hurt me. I will rest my palm on your heaving stomach and whisper to you about your strength as you fall asleep.

You will stop smiling. You will spend your days in front of a bright screen, your ears covered in giant headphones. You will use them as a shield against me, to tune me out. You will play football with your thumbs. You will play cricket with your fingers. You will attend concerts on your computer screen. You will not let me bathe you. You will refuse to let our friends visit. You will repeatedly ignore your mother's phone calls. You will continue to prove your masculinity at night. You will not look at me. You will leave purple blotches on my neck. You will read about your disease and then erase the browsing history. You will stay awake, curling inward from the phantom pain in your numb limbs. You will pretend that I am not there, lying awake next to you. Your hands will slide inside your pants at the sight of naked anime characters on your screen. You will thank me for breakfast. You will hate yourself. You will tie my limbs to the bedposts with the straps you ordered on the internet. You will wash your hands in your plate after dinner. Your fingers will close around my throat till I can't smell the cheap latex anymore. You will tell me that you love me. You will pull me to you and rest your head against my swollen belly. You will kiss it. You will tell me that I am your everything.

I will come dangerously close to telling you. I will refrain at the last moment, aware that admitting the truth wouldn't change what has already occurred. I will stare at my reflection in the mirror, counting the purple patches on my skin. I will not risk you leaving me upon learning the truth. I will believe that you can't live without me, and I can't live without you, so I will wait patiently, month after month, for the real you to resurface. I will walk out of the door – light, free. I will take my time, deliberating over different brands of soap to buy. I will always come back to you. I will wear my brightest smile; the smile I learned from you, when you were you. I will cherish your good days, when we will watch cricket together. I will clutch you by your armpits and pull you on to the toilet seat. I will conceal the marks on my neck with make-up. I will pull you up from the floor, back on the bed. I will wait for you. I will look at you touching yourself to anime characters. I will clutch my belly. I will realize that I lost you a long time ago, to a miracle. I will ruffle your hair. I will kiss your lips. I will walk out of the door – light, free.

Good for Nothing

When the light turns green and I begin to accelerate, my scooter lets out a familiar, dull growl. I draw comfort from this familiarity as I feel the worn-out rubber handles under my palms. I indicate left, check the rear-view mirror and wait for an opening to turn. My reflection stares back at me. I look like a child in my round yellow helmet, a thin cotton scarf draped around my face and neck, with only my eyes showing, like a cocoon, in a puny attempt at insulating myself from heat and dust.

Heat and dust don't frighten me. Nothing that's not a part of me has that ability. I'm only afraid of what's inside of me. My memories, my nightmares, the incompetence of my body, the fear of history repeating itself.

We got excited too early the first three times. The first time we didn't just get our hopes up, we didn't even consider another possible outcome. We took it for granted, as if it was a sure-shot thing. We were reasonably young and in good health, so if we tried to have a baby, we would have a baby. End of story. *Not* end of story. The story didn't end that way. The story ended with us having three miscarriages within the frame of nineteen months.

The first time I miscarried, we were shocked. We froze, became alert, processed what had happened. Then we read about it. We found out that among women who are aware that they are pregnant, about one in eight pregnancies end in miscarriage and manymore miscarriages happen before a pregnancy is even discovered. The doctor couldn't give us a reason for my miscarriage. It's just something that happened. She also did not give us any reason to stop trying.

We didn't recover from the second miscarriage that quickly. Only 2 per cent of women experience two pregnancy losses in a row. We were an anomaly. This was out of the ordinary. It took us far longer to move on from that. When we did, Talha did it with care and hesitation, I did it with a vengeance. I was terrified and a burning need to prove something festered within me – a bad combination.

The third loss shattered me. Only about 1 per cent of women experience three consecutive pregnancy losses. I was in the 1 per cent. Talha and I spent innumerable nights awake in bed together, our hearts aching, bodies curled into each other, protecting and protected.

The doctor told us that my body was suffering. It needed rest, proper recovery. She told us to wait. That news didn't have any significance. It didn't affect our plan, because we didn't have a plan. We weren't even thinking about *next time*. We were mourning *this time* and the two times before this. We clung to each other to survive, and, if we succeeded, that survival would be enough for us.

In the end, the loss didn't rip us apart. It fused us together into a unit, strong and unwavering. Our love for each other expanded and filled the holes in our hearts. We cherished each other as the most precious gifts we'd ever had the honour to receive. And that was enough. That was more than what most people have in a lifetime.

And then, there was another gift. My body recognized its presence immediately. I was terrified. I began moving with care; every step I took was deliberate, vigilant. I did all the right things the doctors, books and YouTube videos tell women in their first trimester to do. I did them without thinking about them, from muscle memory, as a force of habit. I braced myself for the impending doom, and spared Talha. I had to suffer, but if I could protect him, I had to do so. I owed it to the person I loved the most.

Only, things went differently this time. I waited for the doom, but it never came. Now, on my way back from the hospital, where the gynaecologist confirmed that the baby is in perfect health, my mind is buzzing with all that needs to be done. We're out of the risk zone. I can allow my shoulders to slacken, my jaws to unclench, my heart to open up, and accept the joy and hope. If fortune continues to favour us, our family will welcome a precious new member before my thirty-fifth year around the sun.

I am ready to leave the past, with all its gloom and suffering, behind and start anew. I hadn't expected to feel this way, so the moment this thought hits me, I am taken by surprise. I didn't think there was that much in my past that I needed to leave behind. Until this moment, I had thought I already had moved on from those things.

There's a lot I need to do in these six months before my due date. Talha is travelling for work, so the good news will have to wait till he comes home in four days. I can't bear to tell him over the phone. After everything we've gone through, all the difficult times, we deserve a happy moment in each other's embrace when I tell him.

We will tell our families together. I will have to talk to my boss at the newspaper and negotiate a maternity leave. We will have to plan for the baby's arrival, accumulate everything it will need. I try to make a list in my head, but there are too many ideas, broken fragments of sentences, spinning around in there. I can't put them in order; not yet. Not till I address the most pressing issue first.

When I reach Navlakha Square, I turn on to Azad Nagar Road, towards Jyoti's house, hoping I could borrow her car. Depending on how difficult the task at hand proves to be, I might even need Jyoti to come with me and help. I hope she's home and available to help me abduct a grown man and hide him away in my bedroom.

❦

'Aunty Ji, *sab theek hai*. All is well. You don't worry about me. Talha will be back very soon,' I say as nonchalantly as I can. 'Thank you for bringing this ... dish for me. Did you say it's *gatte ki sabzi*? Is *gatta* a vegetable?'

My neighbour, who is appropriately distracted by that foolish question, guffaws. 'Hey bhagwan! No, it's not a vegetable, it doesn't grow on trees! Gatta is made from *besan.* The way to do it is you take besan and mix in spices like *heeng, haldi, dhaniya* and *mirchi* powder. You can also put *ajwain*, but I don't like the taste personally, so I *toh* skip it. Then you mix it together with water …'

As she gives me the step-by-step recipe of gatte ki sabzi, a dish I've cooked a hundred times, I slowly lead her in the direction of the front door. The layout of my flat is quite unusual. It's built in the shape of a square. You enter through the front door into a small room with four more doors. The wall directly in front has two doors, one leading to the living room and the other to the bedroom. To the left is the kitchen and to the right is the bathroom. All the rooms are really small, but I'm thankful for the privacy the walls offer, which makes it feel like we have more space than we actually do.

I rest my hand on Aunty Ji's back and lead her from the kitchen to the entrance, away from the bedroom. She chirps happily about the amount of oil and curd needed to achieve the perfect gatta consistency, and I smile and nod along politely.

'That doesn't sound too difficult,' I comment, just to have something to say.

'No, no, not hard at all. You'll get it the first time only, *pakka se*, absolutely. Don't worry. And if you have questions, you can just knock on my door right here!' She laughs good-naturedly.

'How convenient!' I force my smile to not be as tight, as I look at the distance between my door and hers. They are far too close. Our flats are far too small. Everyone knows what goes on in everyone else's lives every day. If I have to keep her ignorant about the presence of a tied-up man in my bedroom, I have to be extra vigilant.

❧

'*Kam se kam* you can untie my hands at least. This situation is just cruel.' Amir's back slumps against the headboard as he grumpily glares at me when I walk into the bedroom carrying a plate of food.

'I will untie you when you prove to me that you deserve to be set free,' I say merrily. I set the plate in front of him on the bed. I tear a piece of roti, dip it in the gatte ki sabzi and carry it to his mouth. As inconvenient as the uninvited guest had been, I'm actually quite pleased that I didn't have to cook today. The overwhelming smells in the kitchen have been difficult for me to endure since the pregnancy. This wasn't something I had experienced in my first three pregnancies, and I take the new symptom as a good sign. I look for good signs all day; I can't help it.

'Are you serious? You are going to feed me with your hands? Just untie me.' Amir looks in disbelief from me to the bedpost. With Jyoti's help, I had carried him to the bed and tied his wrists together with a rope. Then, for extra security, I tied them to the bedpost. I know that he won't hurt me, that's not what I'm worried about. I'm worried about him hurting himself, or finding a way to run away. If he runs away this time, I can't think of a way to save him. Soon, I will be too pregnant. And once I have a baby to care for … I don't know what to expect.

This is my last chance to pull my elder brother out of the pit he fell into a long time ago, and never found a way to climb out of. Over the years, I've made many failed attempts. In hindsight, they were feeble. I had chosen not to confront the true cause of his ailment; I had chosen to focus on the symptoms instead, and tried to fix them. It was easier that way, more manageable. But it hadn't worked. This time, I'm determined to do whatever it takes. Everyone we know has written him off as a good-for-nothing burden on our parents and society. People love to bad-mouth him and *worry* about him, loudly and without inhibition. But I know who he is. I know what he's made of. I'm made of the same fabric.

'Yes, I'll spoon-feed you, if that's what it takes,' I say firmly, holding the gatte ki sabzi wrapped in a bite of roti in front of his mouth.

Amir leans forward and eats it. Despite his resistance, it's clear to me that he's hungry. When did he last have real food? Does he just survive on Old Monk and *ganja*? I wouldn't be surprised if the only food he ever encounters are the peanuts and *sev* he eats as *chakhna* or nibbles.

Once I finish feeding him what's on the plate, I lift a glass of water and hold it to his lips. I tilt the steel glass, and he gulps down the water. He reeks of alcohol. It's still in his system. It'll be gone soon enough. 'One more roti?' I ask hopefully.

Amir shakes his head. 'This is more food than I've eaten all year. As you can see.' He points to his body with his chin. The skin on his arms is hanging against his bones. Whatever muscles he once had, built over a decade of playing cricket, have melted away with the alcohol abuse. He has dark, deep shadows underneath his eyes, a hollow face hidden behind a scruffy grey beard and moustache. Up close, as I study my brother's face, he seems unfamiliar. This is not the face I have known my whole life, the person I grew up with. My heart is caught in my throat. I feel like I might choke on my own breath.

Amir looks away. We've never been good at confronting emotions. Which is why it was easier for me to abduct him and lock him in a room than talk to him.

'So, what's the plan here? How long are you going to keep me prisoner?' he asks in a nonchalant tone that I can see through.

'As long as it takes.'

'As long as it takes for what? I hate to break it to you, *meri pyari behna*, but there's no saving me. Trust me, I've tried.' He lets out a dry chuckle.

'I don't believe that,' I say, as my heart sinks. I have to grow a thick skin if I have any real hope of saving him from himself. The pregnancy hormones don't help. But at least I have experience and determination. Last time, he ran away because I had tied his hands together, but not to the bedpost. This time, I've thought everything through. I've read as much as I could about alcohol withdrawal, I've removed sharp objects from the room, moved the TV to the bedroom so Amir has some stimulation. I am prepared to watch for the withdrawal symptoms. I've read about people who were so addicted to alcohol that they died from withdrawal. I won't let that happen to Amir. I'll be watching him, ready to call Dr Mishra from the clinic if required.

'You're in for a disappointment,' Amir mutters. There's that word. Everyone loves to use that word for him. I'm sick of it. This will not be a disappointment. I don't care about what people say, but I will not let him disappoint himself this time.

'Then so be it,' I say swiftly as I get up. 'See you at dinner.'

§

To his credit, Talha isn't as surprised as I had expected him to be when he comes home to find the bedroom occupied by a smelly, grumpy lump that is my brother.

'You're back.'

Talha turns at the sound of my voice. He smiles at me and shakes his head. 'We're looking at another cold turkey then?'

'I'm sorry I didn't tell you!'

'Are you really?' He tilts his head, questioningly.

'No,' I say softly. He reaches for me and I melt into his arms. He smells like himself, a smell I have missed in the few days that he was away. My heart is bursting at the seams, holding the good news inside me. 'Come with me,' I say, pulling him to the living room.

Talha turns to close the bedroom door and Amir calls out, 'Good to have you back, Jiju. You can be in charge of tying and untying me every time I have to go to the bathroom now.'

'Looking forward to it,' Talha says, as I lead him to the living room. Talha points to the small *divan* against the wall and says, 'That's our bed indefinitely, I presume?'

I nod distractedly, my heart racing. The memories of previous disappointments are fresh and sharp. For a moment, I question whether I should even share the news with Talha. My heart still cannot fully fathom that the baby is healthy and safe. My lower lip trembles despite my attempts to control myself. Hot, unshed tears hurt the inside of my nose.

'Hey, hey, hey, what's wrong?' Talha cradles my face in his hands. 'Are you worried about Amir? I know it's scary. I'm worried too. But I'm here now, so you don't have to do this alone.'

His warmth and concern are more than I can handle; I burst out crying. 'It's not that ...' I manage to get out between sobs. 'It's not about Amir. Just ... give me a second.'

After holding me patiently for several minutes as I sob in his arms, Talha asks, 'What is it? Barkha?'

I peel myself off my husband's chest and sniff. 'Don't worry. It's good news,' I say.

Talha waits expectantly for me to continue.

I raise my eyebrows. 'Talha, it's *good news*.'

Comprehension dawns in his eyes. His lips stretch into a smile that retreats just as quickly. 'Is it ...? What if ...?' His face is frigid with concern. He clears his throat and speaks carefully, 'When did you find out? How long has it been? Have you been to a doctor yet? We have to be really *really* careful in the first trimester.'

All the grief from our previous losses surfaces on Talha's face. I reach out and stroke his beard. 'It's okay. It's different this time. I'm already in my second trimester. The doctor says everything is as it should be and there's no need to worry about—'

Before I can finish, Talha pulls me in his arms. I feel his body rise and fall with the force of his deep, troubled breathing. I hold him tighter, leaning on him as much as supporting him. *This time, it will be different,* I promise myself. Different for all of us. Talha, Amir and me.

🌹

'Someone hold him down,' Dr Mishra says in a clipped, urgent tone, speaking loudly over Amir's screams. 'Hold his right arm in place. Don't let it shake at all.'

'What's happening? What's happening?' I cry, even as I know that I should keep my mouth shut and stay out of the way. I shouldn't distract the doctor trying to save my brother's life.

'He's dehydrated. Electrolyte imbalance and possible Vitamin-B deficiency.'

I cannot find anything comforting in his flat, sterile tone to cling to. Amir struggles under my grip, groans in agony, and I press down on him harder. He loses consciousness, leaving us in sudden silence. A chill travels down my spine. I look at Talha, who's busy following orders, focused on doing whatever the doctor asks him to do. Soon, two nurses join us. I look at every face around me, before quietly slipping out of the room.

First, I go to the bathroom to vomit. Then, to the kitchen to take a long sip of cold water, then to the living room, to sit down on the *divan*, stroke the baby in my belly and listen to the voices coming from the bedroom. Eventually, the voices subside. I meet this makeshift medical care team at the entrance. It is dark and silent, way past midnight. The city is asleep, and so were we, when I was awakened by the sound of Amir choking.

Before I can say anything, Dr Mishra holds up his hand. 'You did everything right. You called me as soon as you could, and that saved Amir's life tonight.'

'But ... but ... I'm the one who put his life in danger. I locked him up, made him go cold turkey ...' I gasp. My throat is parched.

'You didn't slowly taper off his alcohol intake?' Dr Mishra asks sharply.

'Yes, yes, I did. I gave him less and less alcohol every day, like you said ... But then, since it's been over a month, I stopped giving him any. He hasn't had a drop in ... ten days. Eleven days. He's been locked in there for a month and a half ...' My mind races, as I try to count back the days and narrow it down to the exact day I stopped giving him any alcohol.

'Well, then you did everything right. I should've come to check on him earlier ... I'll do that now. I'll check on him every evening after I close my clinic.'

I nod fervently.

'Thank you, doctor,' Talha says. His eyes are wide. I want to cry just thinking about him, awakened from his sleep, put through a rigorous, heart-wrenching medical emergency. We've gone through this together too many times. He continues, 'Is there anything we should be doing differently? What happened?'

'This was expected. It wasn't out of the ordinary. Amir has never made it this far in his recovery from alcohol addiction, so you can imagine how much of a shock it must be to his system. He needs more care than ever before. I can come here to monitor his vital signs every day and help his body go through the detox. But …' Dr Mishra looks from Talha to me.

'What is it?' I whisper, my heart sinking.

'You have to monitor his mental health status. That's equally important. I don't know how spiritual you are, but I look at it this way: a body is just a shell our soul resides in. I can keep the body healthy, give it everything it needs. But we are not just our bodies.' Dr Mishra pauses. For the first time tonight, his voice holds compassion as he says, 'If you truly hope for Amir to recover, and never relapse … if you want him to get better, he needs help with his mental health. I will prescribe him sleeping pills, and even antidepressants and painkillers as required, but that's only a part of it.'

My jaws clench.

'Thank you, Dr Mishra,' Talha says.

'Welcome. I'll come back for a check-up tomorrow after 6 p.m.' Dr Mishra looks at me one last time, then leaves with the two nurses.

While Talha goes to lock the door behind them, I lay my palm over the baby and tiptoe into the bedroom. In the dull light of the 10-watt bulb in the bedroom, Amir's face glows with sweat. I sit down on the bed next to him and wipe his forehead with my cotton dupatta. Talha peeks in from the door.

'It's not easy,' I say, grinding my teeth. Confronting Amir's mental health also means confronting my own mental health, something I haven't done in fifteen years. We are a sweep-it-under-the-rug type of family. It's the only way we know how to do things.

Talha steps into the bedroom and begins cleaning up. He doesn't say anything, because he doesn't need to. Sometime later, once we've made sure that Amir is comfortable and everything is where it's supposed to be, I lie down on the bed next to him, to keep an eye on him. Talha brings a blanket from the living room, unfurls it on the floor of the bedroom and lies down on his makeshift bed.

🌹

I wait till Talha leaves for his office the next day before going to Amir with a glass of nimbu pani, with the intention of doing what Dr Mishra had advised me to do the night before. My hands shake as I set down the steel glass with the lemon water with a clink on the table next to the bed.

'Thanks for finally untying me,' Amir says bitterly. His voice comes out as a low, raspy breath. The distress he went through last night is apparent in his voice, his face, the defeat in his eyes.

Unable to contain the thoughts that have been crowding my brain since last night, eager to get it out in the open, I blurt out, 'You can't die.'

'Good thing I didn't. Even though you came close to killing me last night.'

'Shut up. I'm serious. You can't die. I can't handle it.'

'Okay. If you can't tell, I'm trying. What do you want me to do? You literally have me locked up in here. What else can I possibly do to appease you?' He speaks with annoyance, but there isn't any malice in his words.

'I need you to let it go. Forget about what happened and move on. It's been fifteen years,' I say evenly. I have the words arranged and ready.

Amir freezes. If there's one thing that's remained consistent ever since the incident, it's that we never talk about it. It's for good reason. It doesn't lead anywhere, so we leave that can of worms unopened. It has reached a point where if I don't talk about it, I might lose my brother forever. That's the only thought that gives me the courage to say what I say next.

'It happened to me, but I know it was harder for you.' I can't bear to look into his wounded eyes. I look away, at the floor. 'But, Bhai, I was able to move on. It took me a long time. I spent years and years in the depths of depression. Only, I was high-functioning. I masked it, held my head high, carried on. You didn't see me whenever I was alone. I would cry myself to sleep every night. I would be in physical pain from carrying the memories of the night I was attacked.'

'Raped.'

My eyes dart to his, taken aback. My mouth opens, but I can't speak.

'If you're so over it, so *moved on*, as you put it, then you can at least say the word.'

It's okay. I'm okay. He's lashing out because he's in pain. I take a few shallow breaths, and say, 'I never said that I'm over it. I can never be over it. But I've tried my best to forget it. Pushed the memories away every time they resurface. And trust me, they resurface plenty of times. Just because I push them away, and never talk about what happened, doesn't mean I don't still suffer, that I don't still feel scared when I walk alone in the dark, that I don't have nightmares and I don't—'

'I'm sorry, I'm sorry,' Amir says, looking genuinely remorseful. 'I didn't mean to say—'

'No, we *have to* say things. We have to get it out in the open. It's been long enough! If we don't, you will quite literally die, if not from alcohol poisoning then from kidney failure or depression or self-harm or a hundred other things I'm terrified of every day. And I will never recover from it. If we don't talk about it now, we are both done. It's just a matter of time. One way or another, it will kill us both.' As I say it, I realize the gravity of my words.

'I don't *want* to die! Don't you think that if I wanted to die, I wouldn't be here right now? I would've been long gone. But I'm here, every day, tied to this bed, locked in this room, depending on my younger sister to feed me, my brother-in-law to look after me. I must be costing you so much money.

The doctor and medicines and everything. Especially now, with the baby coming …'

'How do you know about the baby?' I ask, taken by surprise.

'Oh, please. I'm neither completely blind nor that self-involved that I wouldn't notice that I'm about to have a baby niece or nephew.'

'Then be there for your little niece or nephew. Move on from the past. You can't let it govern your life and come in the way of—'

'It's not that easy! Don't you think I've tried? It's easy for you to say it's in the past, but it's not. Not for me. I relive it every single day. I sank so deep …' Amir shakes his head. His forehead is lined with the wrinkles of a much older man. At thirty-six, he looks ten years older. Grief and alcohol have fed on him for years, leaving him a hollow shell. 'It was all I thought about, every waking minute. For years and years. Revenge and fury and *what ifs* and a hundred other questions. I thought about it so much that it's become a part of me. I can never get rid of it. Sometimes, if I try really hard, I can go a whole day without thinking about it, but then I fall asleep. And my nightmares take me right back there … finding you, too late. Don't you think there's a reason I prefer passing out? At least then I don't dream.'

I remember how Amir's world had changed forever that night. It was his friend who had raped me. It was through Amir that he had got close enough to me to rape me. Amir had found me, and never forgiven himself for any of it: asking me to take admission in his college, making me move to Indore from our small town, sending his friend to pick me up from a party one night. He must know that it wasn't his fault, he didn't do anything. But he has taken the blame for it from the beginning. He has never let himself off the hook. He dropped out of college after that, in his third year. I was only in my first year, and I continued, holding my head high. Doing anything else would've given my assaulter more power. I had been determined.

Amir had dealt with his grief differently. He had let it fill his heart, his soul. He had lived in it. Ever since we were kids, he had taken the role of the protector very seriously. No matter what the circumstance, it was a big brother's responsibility to protect his little sister. After this incident, he had decided that he was a failure and never recovered from that belief.

No one knew about the rape, but there were rumours about something. Something significant enough to make a student in his final year of college flee. Because that's what he did, my rapist. He disappeared. Then Amir dropped out and I stayed. No one could understand why; if something had happened to me, and I was okay, should my brother be so broken? Over the years, he's been ostracized, considered a useless drunk with no job, no college degree, nothing to contribute. Our own parents have treated him like an outcast ever since his first depressive episode.

What they don't understand is that I had to suppress everything and move on, to survive. Over the years, I let it resurface slowly, dealt with the mountain of despair in pieces. Amir, on the other hand, felt it all at once. He let it shatter him, and could never glue the pieces back together. As I look at him now, all I see is the twenty-one-year-old young man whose life I changed forever, for the worse. I put a hand on his arm. 'I didn't know about your nightmares.'

'You never asked.'

'I couldn't! I couldn't go back there. I had to leave that place. There's nothing for me in my past. I can only focus on my present and my future. That's the only way I know how to survive. I have nightmares too; I have those memories that resurface … but I can't let them live in my head. I have to push them away.'

'And I'm happy that you can. I'm happy that you survived. Your happiness, what you have now with Talha and the baby – that's more than I could've ever asked for my little sister.' Amir speaks with such tenderness that a sob escapes my lips. I sit down next to him.

'But I want *you* too. I need you to be okay. Nobody can replace you. You're my brother,' I say gently, tears streaming down my face. 'Please, please.'

'I don't know how to promise that … I'm really trying.'

'And that's okay. That's enough for now. Just promise me that you will keep trying. That's all I'm asking. I know it's so hard, but please, just keep trying. We're here for you. We'll help you at every step. And soon, there will be a little niece or nephew to play with. Things will get better, brighter.'

Amir is silent. I can't think of anything to say. I don't know if saying anything can even help. It can't be that easy. But I try. 'You know … I never told anyone … but for the last two years, I have been feeling like I'm being punished. I … I had three miscarriages, and I couldn't shake the feeling that it was what I deserved ... for what we did ... the abortion.'

Amir looks up at me, shaken out of his thoughts. 'Don't say that! It's not your fault. You couldn't possibly have had that monster's baby. I don't regret taking you to that clinic one bit. In fact, it's the one useful thing I've done for you in my life. The one thing I don't regret.'

Emotions overwhelm me, crashing inside me like wild waves. I succumb to them. Dropping my head on his shoulder, I let the tears come. 'You have done so much,' I say after I regain a semblance of composure. 'But I need more from you now. Now that I finally have a baby to look forward to ... it feels like I might be able to turn a page. Come with me to the other side. I can't go there without you. We're tied in this together. I can only be okay if you're okay.'

'I'm trying.' Amir looks defeated.

'That's all I ask. Just try. Because for a moment there ... it felt like you weren't trying. That you don't want to be okay.'

'Misery feels safe. I built a home there. Hope, on the other hand, is brutal,' he says sadly, honestly. 'Every time I slip, it cuts like a knife. I *have* tried, you know. So many times over the years. I've tried my best, but it's not enough.'

'It doesn't matter! It doesn't matter if your best isn't enough. We also have my best, and Talha's. That's triple the impact. It'll be more than enough.' I laugh, trying to lighten the mood. Amir doesn't join in. I speak seriously, 'I know that it's not easy. But we're here for you, as long as it takes.'

Amir nods weakly. I wipe the tears off his cheeks and rest my forehead against his. 'We're in this together,' I murmur. 'We're in this together.'

Amir's head collapses on my shoulder, as his whole body convulses.

'You're not alone. I'm not going anywhere.' I hold him, cry with him.

'We're in ... this together.' Amir somehow manages to string the words between shudders.

'Yes. We're in this together,' I say with a rush of determination. This is going to be a long fight, but we're on our way. It'll get a little easier, with Amir on the same side as us, not fighting us every step of the way. It's good to be on the same team for a change, united against a common enemy.

We stay there like that for a while, till our tears dry and our strength is replenished. Then, I rise slowly. Straightening my kurti, I say slowly, 'It was only five minutes for him. But it's a lifetime for us. We can't erase it, but we can try to make it small, shove it away into a dark corner. He has taken so much from me already, don't let him take you too.'

As I walk out of the bedroom, I leave the door behind me open.

Real

Either Pihu came back to the hostel really late last night and then left really early this morning or she didn't come back at all. Most probably the latter. Ever since she and her boyfriend started fucking, I've seen less and less of her. They can fuck all they want but does she really have to stay over and *sleep* with him the whole night too? We get eight 'outs' in a whole semester and even then our local guardian has to come to the hostel and pick us up before we are let out. And, we only get one night out. Every time Pihu has to visit her boyfriend she has to sneak out clandestinely and she could be expelled from the college hostel if she was found out. She once started to tell me the method she employed to get out but I stopped her immediately and asked her to keep me out of it because I don't wanna be an accomplice or anything you know. She's taking so many risks to go see her boyfriend it's insanity. Maybe because it's the honeymooney phase of her 'relationship' that's got her so gushy and like sappy. But whatever. Her life. After her first time she said the sex was good. I've never heard a virgin say that before so of course she was lying that poor sweet girl. She's just so love-struck right now it's hard to watch because it makes me go aww and then wanna puke at the same time. *You cannot believe how gentle and caring he is Gauri. I'm sooo happy.* Pfft. Who the hell wants gentle and caring! Like be a real man and gimme the real thing, you know. Anyway I guess, as long as she's happy. It's actually for the best that Pihu isn't home because now I can lie in bed for another hour and do whatever the fuck I want without her sitting there at her desk and judging me for wasting time. I am a very very ambitious girl and Pihu is actually the only person in the whole world who has ever accused me of something like this. I know she means it as a joke when she says *your life will pass you by while you nap* but what the hell. I don't owe her anything and she's no one to dictate how I spend my days. People like her just irk me. They don't even realize that they're a sad product of capitalism who have bought into the idea of productivity and they truly believe they have to hustle hard every second of every day in order to be doing enough to quench their thirst for fulfilment and meaning. Simple-minded people who have been on the wrong track all along. When she's not spending nights with her boyfriend she goes to bed before midnight and wakes up at like 7 in the morning and immediately starts studying. By the time I wake up at like 11 she has already studied for a few hours and returned from the gym too. Who does that. Sometimes I think she does all this super-organized and punctual shit just to annoy the fuck out of me. Like to highlight the contrast between the two of us. I don't know. She's a sweet person though. Whenever she cooks, she makes extra for me and keeps it in one of our cheap plastic containers. She never puts it in the mini fridge though. I don't know why. Why someone would leave food out during summer when it's so hot is beyond me but maybe she does it so I will wake up early and eat before the food spoils, but that's just stupid because I could just wake up and put the food in the fridge and go back to sleep. Once she made these awesome chutney sandwiches early in the morning and I smelled them on my way to the bathroom because, of course, she had just left them on the counter and the chutney was ruining the bread so I ate the sandwiches. I wasn't able to fall back asleep and was irritated with everything all day because of my lack of sleep, but at least the sandwiches were good. All food is good actually and Pihu is such a wonderful cook too. Our stupid college doesn't even have one half-decent cook, I tell you. Our college is so pretentious. It *aims to be an institution of excellence dedicated to producing leaders of the future* but the food fucking sucks. I didn't bust my ass studying to get a scholarship and come here for this. We had to take charge of the situation, so Pihu and I sneaked in a small stove and it's been such a lifesaver really. But there's no food this morning because Pihu's busy fucking her boyfriend. I hate how these girls make such a big deal of sex. We're in the first year of college and, like, once we graduate, we're gonna be out in the real world, which means we'll meet loads of boys anyway. So, what's the rush right. I don't get it. These girls are just so depraved it's gross. I've been bunking classes and sleeping in a lot lately. Today is

Sunday so that's okay but I need to get my shit together. Finals are so fucking close it's scary. I need to build my Twitter account too. I've got to tweet more regularly and get more engagement in order to keep building my following. If I am serious about getting into JNU after finishing college it's high time I get serious about this it's no joke. My English teacher is very happy with my essays, so that's good. I feel like she's the only person with brains around here. Everyone else is a sucker for whatever's new and selling, everything superficial. But I get it. I'm on my way to becoming a part of the whole popular culture thing too. At least I'm trying. My Twitter account is the first step towards that. I should probably check on it though. I do it first thing every morning before getting out of bed. Pihu may think I'm being lazy but I'm actually working on my career already at nineteen while she's all wide-eyed about her stupid boyfriend so what does she know. I touch the blue bird on my screen to find two new notifications on my Twitter. A like and a follow. Yay this is so exciting! Just what I needed to start my day off. I've had this account for over a year now and I have twenty-one followers. Twenty-two including this one. I get a follower like one or two times a month, so this is a big deal. I'm nothing yet, you know. Just a teenager with thoughts like every other teenager but I am going to stand out of the crowd soon everyone will see. I should post something new today for my new follower. Not *for* him like directly of course, because that would be stupid. I did that one time when someone followed me – I don't even remember his name now – but after that post he and two more people unfollowed me so I deleted the welcome tweet and haven't done anything like that again.

Pihu and I decided we will use the walls next to the other's bed to put up posters and shit. I used to have this picture of me and Mom on my side but I couldn't fucking see it and it didn't make sense. So last week I moved it to the wall on Pihu's side of the room and now I can see it all the time. It's making me a little sick to think that Mom can see me lying in bed instead of studying. My parents are all about studies, you know. Not that they could've ever dreamed to afford to send me to a college like this on their own. I worked super hard and got the scholarship here and when I finish college I'll probably leave this town for Delhi. But it is the good kind of scary because I am excited too. I put up the poster I ordered from Monika Sen's merch site on Pihu's wall as well. It's *so* good. Monika Sen is, like, my most favourite writer. She's just everything. She's so pretty and successful and famous and so fucking talented. I love her writing and everything else she does. I'll be like her one day. It's not even like she's a listless clueless *artist* who's stuck in the circle of being lost and trying to find herself in her writing; no. She's a very smart businesswoman. She runs this organization for teenagers which is like a forum and so cool and also her powerful young adult fiction following ensures she sells loads and loads of merchandise through her website. God … I wanna be like her. She has everything and she's only a few years older than me. That's what has inspired me to start early you know. Everyone's starting early and getting famous young now. If you don't have 1 million followers on social before twenty-five, you're basically a failure. I have to really get my head in the game and complete my manuscript and build a following through my Twitter too, so that I can be as awesome as Monika Sen by the time I'm her age. She started off at twenty, so I've already got a one-year head start on her. I'm not saying it will be easy but I know I'll make it. What I've learned from Monika Sen is that a writer isn't just her writing, she is everything else that surrounds her too. It's the personality that is built around her name. I have to be that person people would want to idealize. My phone's battery is low; I need to plug it in. I should probably get up and go downstairs to workout too. Lose those extra pounds and get back in shape you know. People say it's hard to lose weight but I don't buy it. It's just a matter of a few weeks and if you are determined you can do anything. Eating clean and moving your body, that's it; it's not that big a deal. I put my phone down and look for the charger but can't find it. I need a new one. I think it's a sign that I should get a new phone. This one's battery drains out in like three hours, this stupid thing. I think the universe is sending me signs for the whole past week to get a new phone. First, I think it's giving me carpal tunnel and then I dropped it in class and the screen pretty much shattered and now I cannot find the fucking charger. These are definitely signs. Pihu lost her virginity a few weeks ago and can't stop talking about sex, which is depressing because how much control are you going to give a boy over you? I think Ranjit is cute and by the way he looks at me, I can tell that there's definitely like a pull there. But I don't know. Who knows with boys. I should probably check if he tweeted something today. I doubt it because he's one of the cool guys and people like that have late Saturday nights and no Sunday mornings. Especially the ones with girlfriends, I suppose. He hasn't tweeted anything. His last tweet is a video of a cat trying to catch fish under ice. The stupid creature has no idea what ice is and it's just so hilarious I laugh every time I watch it. I get another notification on my Twitter. This is so great; such a great start to the day. It's a wonderful feeling to connect with people online. They have no *real-life* connection with you but you're still so connected through the content you share and the conversations you engage in. I try to generate very funny and fresh content on my Twitter to fit the current trend of low attention span. Why the fuck can people not pay attention for a few minutes and concentrate on something is beyond me, but yeah okay. I give them what they want. A one-liner, a photo, a meme, a quote, nothing too long ever. This comment on my post is stupid. People are so fucking retarded it's ridiculous how stupid people can be. I am going to delete this comment and block this girl right now. I don't know who people think they are. Like, it isn't even funny how much they can intrude in your life without realizing that they are overstepping their boundaries and breaching your privacy. Fuck this, I need to get up and go to the gym now. It's after 12 and I'm getting hungry. Going to the gym in the morning is the most ideal because then you can just have some milk or fruit juice or something and just go right away. But now I would need to eat something because I haven't had anything to eat in like twelve hours and I wouldn't be able to workout properly because I will have no energy. I think I should cook something. I don't cook as well as Pihu does and I miss her. I'll just have some bread with marmalade or wait, we had Maggi didn't we? Pihu doesn't like it when I have Maggi for breakfast so lucky me that she's not here right now. She can be such a mom sometimes. Refined flour is bad for you, I know, but we're only having it every once in a while so it's really not the end of the world. I put the laptop on my study table and pull out the stove from under Pragati's bed. I have to wash the big bowl before I can cook Maggi. Ugh, going out in the corridor and to the shared bathroom is the worst. I don't want people staring at me and my dirty bowl this early in the morning. Someone ratted out the girls in Room 807 to the warden once and then there was random checking and they found a half-empty bottle of Old Monk inside a sock in 807 and since then hostel security has been kind of tight. We cannot afford to lose our stove, not just because we won't get to make our own food, but also because Papa hasn't been sending me a lot of money lately. It sucks to be a small business owner because sometimes you have a lot of money but you don't get to spend it because you are preparing for the days when you'll need it for when you'll have little to no money, which is like always, so yeah. I would like to have a well-paying stable job instead any day. I do need to get more active on my Twitter. The last time I tweeted something was like a week ago. I want to be present and visible always but good subject matter is the most important thing to me. That's one thing I refuse to compromise on. This early in my career I do need to be very careful because I have to be a smart businesswoman like Monika Sen. Soon enough Gauri Bafna will be as famous and rich as Monika Sen. It'll happen. My manuscript is almost done. Penguin rejected it and HarperCollins and Westland but that's okay. If they hadn't in fact I would've lost respect for them, because my novel was shit. The draft that I sent them was like the first thing I'd written in my life and it was literal garbage. Since then I've learned so much, read so much. I've read all Monika Sen's books and then rewritten my whole book. She gets it, you know. She gets her readers and she gives them what they want from her and she makes her content her own and that is what I need to do too. That's how I need to build myself. I had sent my book proposal to her publishing start-up too but they emailed to let me know that it wasn't the right fit for them. The girl in the hallway gives me a weird look but I keep walking. It doesn't take me long to clean the bowl, I just run it under the shower in one of the stalls in the bathroom I have to share with twenty other girls on the floor. That's one thing about this college I'm not going to miss at all. I've stopped drinking water after 8 p.m. now because it sucks to get up and walk all the way out here to pee in the middle of the night. Since I am here I might as well pee but it's difficult holding a bowl so I keep it on the flush tank for a minute. Pihu wouldn't approve of things like that, she's such a clean freak it's torture. Logic says that only the bottom of the bowl is touching the flush tank so there's nothing to worry about. I pick up the bowl and take it back to the room. It's too sunny and warm outside, it's better with curtains pulled. I wonder when Pihu will be back. It takes five minutes for Maggi to cook, not two like it says on the pack. Fucking liars but I don't really mind because Maggi is the best thing that ever happened to me. It is my survival food; I have to have it at least once a day it's so good. I eat it hungrily but it's too hot and tastes terrible because I haven't brushed my teeth but I know it will get better on the second-third bite like it always does. This poster is amazing. It has a quote from one of Monika Sen's books on it. *Better put on a happy face than a gloomy one if we have to go through life anyway. Attitude is what defines our journey through the bumpiest of roads.* I had to ask my friend in Mumbai to get it from a store that was selling a limited number of signed posters and then he couriered it over to me. I still can't believe I have Monika Sen's signature for real. It was so great of her to take the time for her fans. I touched every millimetre of the poster as soon as I got it just so I could touch the same piece of paper that Monika Sen's fingers had held. This lady is everything I wanna be. Girls look up to her and guys go mad over her, what else could she need? I just need to lose a little weight. I will have to wait before heading downstairs because I've just eaten a bowlful of Maggi. At least half an hour or maybe one. I should use the time to work on my next tweet. My last tweet was a link to a video with a cat trying to catch fish under ice. So hilarious. I wonder if Ranjit noticed that I retweeted his tweet. I don't think he did though, he's so busy fucking his current girlfriend. Once I am published and famous and successful I won't have to worry about getting attention from boys anymore; I'll get too much of it

actually. Like Monika Sen. I don't think she actually signed
the poster herself. She must be so busy in life you know.
When I reach that stage I know I'm not gonna waste my
energy in such tiny insignificant things. Big picture. Always
the big picture. That's what's important. But this quote really
connects with me. In a weird way I feel like she can read my
exact thoughts. I feel so attached to what she said. I know I
have a long road ahead of me and I have to work really hard
to reach where she is and farther. And I'm taking my steps
towards it with a smile on my face because, like Monika Sen
said, why not. This is too much. I am overwhelmed with
emotion. This is so close and personal and relevant to me;
how could she be reading my thoughts? Did I post this
somewhere and she found it online or does she have access
to my laptop somehow? Well of course she doesn't have
access to my laptop how could she I'm just being ridiculous.
I don't even remember posting this stuff online for her to
have copied from there. But I definitely have it on my laptop
somewhere within the folders and folders of journaling I've
saved in the past several months. It'll take me an eternity to
check so I won't waste my breath because it could be a
coincidence you know. We are so alike as people we could
both just be thinking the same thing it's possible. For now
I should really think about what to post next on my Twitter.
Or maybe workout first. That is also crucial in becoming a
well-rounded celebrity. Guys wouldn't want to be with me
and girls wouldn't want to be like me if I'm fat. Not that I
am. I've just put on a little bit of weight over the past few
months. I promised myself I will workout every day like a

year ago and I've tried my best but with the pressure of maintaining a relevant Twitter account and at the same time writing a book it's too much some days. The first draft of my manuscript was really bad but I have forgiven myself for it. I had written only three chapters anyway. That's how it works and that's the smart way to do these things. Publishers need three sample chapters, a short synopsis and a brief author bio sort of thing and that's all they need for the first step. If they like your proposal they'll ask you for the rest of the manuscript otherwise they just say no, at which point you can start working on something new, an idea you think would be of interest to the publisher. In my case it was a little different though. I got rejections from the big publishing houses but I'm a sport and took it in my stride. But this is my story and I know this is the story that's gonna get me everything Monika Sen has. I'm working on the same manuscript and it is almost done. I have so many great ideas for it too. I'm going to change the face of it completely and woo the pants off publishers. It just requires a little more work. I won't let the manuscript be the central thing in my career though. I have to always be alert and know when I'm slipping from the big picture by giving too much importance to just one thing. Pihu says I'm pretty and by the way Ranjit looks at me it's fucking evident that he has the hots for me so I know I'm not ugly at all. The Internet says I should ideally be 59 kg based on my height. Just a little weight loss and I'll be like Monika Sen and everything will be perfect. I feel good today. A follower on Twitter, a bowl of Maggi, the funny cat video, not bad at all. I will work on my manuscript today too once I'm back from the gym. I have the whole story in my head, just need to type it is all. I should put on my gym outfit and then tweet something before hitting the gym. I pull out the pink-and-black tank top from under a pile of clothes in the closet. I got it on sale from Adidas they only had sizes XS and L left so I had to get L which was a little tight for me but I figured it would fit me once I started working out. I put it on. The pink looks amazing against my skin for sure. It's riding up my stomach though and I think the stitches are showing because of the stretching on the sides. What the fucking hell? I've definitely not gained this much weight; maybe I got the XS by mistake. I struggle out of the fucking top. These mass-production companies they are all a bunch of idiots. I don't even care anymore, I'll just wear the T-shirt I wore to bed last night, it doesn't matter. I open up my laptop. Maybe I can find the quote that Monika Sen stole from me here. It's impossible for me to read all this in a day, I have so many files and folders it could be anywhere. I could use the find command but I'm sure the bitch switched the words. She's too smart to plagiarize without thought and planning. I'd weigh myself and find out what's going on but I think the scale is broken. It's been showing more and more absurd numbers every time. I was surprised at first a few months ago when it showed 74 all of a sudden and then it showed more more more, then the last time I checked it showed 83 kg. Insane. I'm absolutely certain she didn't sign those posters herself. She isn't the kind of person who would care about her fans enough to do that kind of a gesture. All she cares about is her books selling and making money, that's it. Is this sign even real or is it a stamp? I wouldn't be surprised if it is. If this woman is shameless enough to take credit for someone else's writing she is surely capable of passing off someone's signature as her own. God, Monika Sen disgusts me. I am waiting for responses from publishers. After I received those stupid rejection emails I wrote to them telling some of my plans for the manuscript and that I will send them the newer draft very soon. I haven't heard from them yet. I sent it to eleven. Let's see. I hope they don't lose interest before I am able to send them the finished manuscript. I'm working on it. The fact that I found out that Monika Sen didn't sign the poster herself is a sign. It's a sign that I should expose her. She needs to be cancelled. It's not just that she didn't sign the poster herself but the quote on it is mine, not hers. I need to expose to the world what kind of a sick human being she is. Budding writers need all the help they can get to find their footing in the publishing world and situations like these where one can't send their manuscript to a publisher for the fear of getting plagiarized are just disgusting. I didn't know when I sent in my proposal to her stupid start-up publishing house that she would steal my work, did I. I need to find the quote in my folders immediately. I also need to find which of her books has this quote because without it I have no proof. How can I go to the gym now? I pull out her latest book from my shelf. This one came out a few months ago *after* I'd sent my manuscript. I'm not quite sure what to expect from it. I've read it before and I loved it because I felt so connected with her protagonist and the theme. When I'd found out that her book was about amnesia too I had been surprised in the beginning. I had sent her my proposal just months before that. I remember having wondered what were the odds of that happening. But I had let it go giving her the benefit of the doubt. Things could happen with Ranjit even now but I am nervous mostly because I am not in the best shape of my life. I expect too much of myself and push myself too hard. It's reaching a point where it's unhealthy for me to worry so much about dieting and exercising. Oh my fucking God, this book is exactly the same as mine. This woman has disguised it so well that even I hadn't caught on to it when I had read it for the first time. The similarities are uncanny. Too many and too much to be mere coincidences. How stupid does she think I am? Did she really think I wouldn't find out and she would never be caught. I'm going to mention her in a tweet and ask *@sen_monika hey loved your book Every Single Thing where did you get the concept for that?* Let's see what she says to that. I cannot just go ahead and attack her because then she would be alert; I need to coax it out of her. I will wait for her to reply and do some crunches in the meantime. I am so pumped I cannot settle down I have to do something to release all this energy. I don't want to go back to Twitter just yet because of that dumb guy's dumb comment. I'm on the floor ready to do crunches when I hear a tweet. I jump to see what Monika Sen has to say for herself. It isn't her. Someone retweeted my tweet. I think they misinterpreted it as a real compliment. I can't just sit and wait, I have to do something about this and *now*. I tweet again. *@sen_monika how did you come up with the* *idea of AMNESIA AS THE CENTRAL THEME of the book?* I open the book again to pick out more similarities. *@sen_monika why did you choose FIRST PERSON NARRATION AND PRESENT TENSE specifically?* I flip two pages. *@sen_monika from where did you get the idea of STARTING THE BOOK IN A HOSPITAL?* Holy fuck, this girl really is shameless. She even stole tiny details and not just the plot and theme. *@sen_monika how did you come up with the idea of your character waking up with an OXYGEN MASK on her face in a hospital?* This is too much. This woman needs to be called out on her lies and deceits. *@sen_monika how would you react if you found out that someone has been STEALING YOUR WRITING AND TAKING CREDIT for it?* I need to forget about the creep asking me my cup size on Twitter. I need to focus on this right now. It's a great topic to talk about. I need to get people on my side to form a support system for me. It shouldn't be hard. People hate injustice done towards new artists by established ones. I don't want to write a lot though because I don't wanna talk *around* it and a long post would dilute content matter too. I start a tweet thread and keep typing facts super straightforward that my work has been stolen and I need help getting it back. I conclude my plea with a *Please support me in my fight against plagiarism.* One person retweeted all my tweets to Monika Sen and all my tweets from this thread too. I grab the half-eaten bag of Kurkure from under my desk and dig in. I don't usually eat too much but it just feels like with all this happening to me I should get to eat whatever the fuck I want to. Last night I looked

for indications of pimples on my face but couldn't find any
so maybe that's a sign that I can eat unhealthy oily food
without getting pimples and that's good. I'll start dieting
seriously tomorrow but right now I have to deal with this
fucking thing. I switch to my laptop; too much is going on.
No new updates on Ranjit's Twitter. I wish he would just
dump his girlfriend and come to me you know. Why is he
with her anyway, she's so skinny, she's like a skeleton and
she's not even that pretty he can do so much better. I close
the tab with Ranjit's Twitter profile. He's not posting anything
new which means he's still fucking his girlfriend, I don't
know what the big hype is about sex. Another person
retweeted one of my tweets to Monika Sen. Maybe my tweets
need to be more hard-hitting. I have to come up with
something that's suitable for my situation but at the same
time is universal and retweetable. I shouldn't think too
much, just say it, follow my instincts. It's a sign from the
universe that I need to uncover this otherwise why in a
country of 1.35 billion people would I be the one buying
this book and reading my stolen manuscript; what are the
odds of that happening? It's definitely not a *coincidence* I
hate that word people who keep saying that everything is
coincidence when it's clearly destiny. People need to have
more fucking faith in the way the world works. You can't
just disregard these things simply because your brain is too
small to comprehend the meaning of it. I go to my email
and search for the proposal. There it is, sent on 11/10/19, so
over four months ago. I google the release date of Monika
Sen's book but can't find anything concrete. I go to her

Instagram page and scroll down down down. God she posts so much shit this woman is such an attention-seeker. Her launch pictures finally start showing up. The very first one, the one that happened in Bengaluru, happened on 15 December so like two months ago it adds up. Look at her smiling motherfucker at the camera holding my book in her hands so fucking shamelessly she's so disgusting this is too much. I don't think the quote on the poster is from this specific book actually so it might not be mine. Well even if I didn't have it written down I at least thought it first for sure. What kind of writer does that steal someone else's work and claim it as their own no sense of integrity and being a writer she should know how much work goes into finishing a manuscript how could she do this to another writer. I've been working on my book for so long now and only have three shitty chapters of the first draft to show for it even though I have the entire final draft in my head of course all of it. My writing is really progressing if only I had the time to sit down and type it out that's all. In my head it's a fucking bestseller it will be because I understand the business I know how this works. I wonder when Pihu will be back it's late afternoon now. Monika Sen just tweeted about Valentine's Day what the fuck she's so vain no one wants to know that her V-Day plans include her cooking Chinese food for her single girlfriends or whatever it looks delicious but so what. She stole my shit and now how dare she ignore my tweets and tweet about fucking V-Day like for real is that more important than plagiarism. Nothing should be more important to a writer because it's like actual stealing of thoughts ideas time effort just come up with your own original content you know. If you don't have anything new to say don't say it what gives you the right to copy someone else's work and pass it as your own ludicrous ridiculous insane. *@sen_monika thinks her #ValentinesDay plans are more important than the burning issue of plagiarism. #JusticeforGB #FightAgainstPlagiarism* I take a screenshot of the first page of my manuscript it's not copy-edited so there are some typos shit like that but that's not the point. It's a story about a *girl* who wakes up with *amnesia* in a *hospital* with an *oxygen mask* on her face and is *disoriented* and hears *medical equipment beeping* and figures out she's in a hospital. It's written in *first person* and *present tense* and well I could go on and on about this. All this can't fucking be coincidence. I know what she's going to say she's going to say she hasn't even read my manuscript which is fucking convenient for her I won't let it rest I have to raise a voice against this important issue can't keep silent and endure it anymore. Like the professional I am I am going to write emails to Monika Sen's publisher that published *Every Single Thing* and the start-up where I sent my manuscript. I shouldn't email her directly should I no that won't be appropriate. I'm not going to handle this like an amateur. It's so fucking hot in here I stink I'm fucking worked up this fucking T-shirt sticking to my body. I should take a shower I will take one after my workout. It doesn't make sense to take one now then again after exercising that's fucking retarded. I wonder if sex is actually as good as people think it is. Pihu seems so happy nowadays it's sickening and disgusting. I am composing the emails when I hear another tweet this woman is so fucking unrepentant she's just tweeting random shit ignoring me over and over again as if I do not exist. *@sen_monika are you silent because you have nothing to say because you plagiarized from me? #plagiarism #JusticeforGB* I am starting to get responses now from people I don't know. One person is livid he thinks I'm lying to taint his favourite writer's name the other two believe me are asking for more details. I retweet and favourite their tweets. I'll keep doing that it helps to let them know you're listening and their support is important to you. All I need to do now is take pictures of the first few pages of Monika Sen's book and post both mine and her pages online for everyone to see anyone with half a brain would be able to see that she's a fucking thief. I worked on my manuscript for so long I am not going to let her get away with stealing it no never. The dates add up I mean four months is plenty of time for her to have stolen from me written her book and published it right. She's a professional commercial writer for fuck's sake of course she can do it. I got the idea of amnesia stuck in my head when I read this Sophie Kinsella book *Remember Me* of course *The Bourne Identity* and *Ghajini*. I wanted to explore it further that's why I wrote what I wrote. It's insane that Monika Sen would steal from me. I upload the pictures online. This is escalating now there's only so much stuff I can fit in 140 characters so I keep adding one tweet at a time. I upload everything highlight similarities in yellow mention them in ALL CAPS keep using the hashtags *#JusticeForGB #FightAgainstPlagiarism* I could sue her the truth will come out and she'll be defamed. Papa probably can't afford a lawsuit I can ask. Plagiarism laws are so fucking twisted though with enough money influence she will wriggle her way out of it which is the last thing I need right now. I need to get other people involved. I am not enough I need more people. I have a friend who has 273 followers on his Twitter and he posts book reviews and shit I'm sure he'd be happy to take on this issue and post about this. Maybe even interview me or something that's a brilliant idea. I'll show this bitch what she gets for plagiarizing my content. I hit send on emails to the publishers retweet the rest of the tweets I'm getting I got seven now. I tweet some more *maybe it's a coincidence* one person is saying what a brainwashed moron. I won't entertain that thought for even a minute. Monika Sen chose a female protagonist yeah okay obvious choice she's a girl herself. She chose present tense well that's like one of the two ways to write a book generally. She chose first person narration which could be coincidental but I don't know put together there's just too much similar stuff. What about the fact that her central theme is amnesia and her character wakes up in a hospital with an oxygen mask and beeping sounds and is disoriented at first. I'm not completely stupid I know that taken separately all this sounds like harmless or whatever but the reason her book is selling is because of a mixture of all these things. I've read the fucking reviews on Amazon and people love that she got into the head of her character which I know is because she wrote in first person and argh. There's just too much too much I cannot think of this as a coincidence I cannot back down now I will look like an idiot. Maybe it's not too late there are only a few people responding it's not gone viral yet so she's technically not cancelled yet. I should think this through plagiarism is a big accusation to level against a writer. What if she sues me for defamation or harassment or mental distress or some other shit? Not that I'm backing down because I'm scared or anything because I'm not. I just need to take a deep breath and think this through; what the fuck is the matter with this woman now she's tweeting pictures from her vacation on some island fuck her fuck this I need to take a shower so bad but workout first I need to look good when I'm on television talking about standing up against plagiarism. Fuck the emails I need to take this public. I need more writers involved in this I get up pull on my pants and tie up my hair. I'll show this fucking bitch she can't get away with this. I think my friend with 273 followers would be home I'll ask him to interview me right now would he need a picture I have to look good but wait I can give him that picture of me I use everywhere because my face looks skinny and it's taken under the sun so the lighting is perfect and makes me seem fairer than I am and my dirty brown eye colour pops for a change. I can see that picture plastered all over news channels when they cover this yes great that's perfect. I can write a book about this experience too people would love to read that and it could be my debut novel after my intended debut novel got stolen wow that would be so awesome media would jump to grab that story. It wouldn't be a novel it would be an autobiography and it's going to be spectacular it takes courage to raise your voice against these biggies you know. Maybe I should post something about bullying it'll get a lot of retweets I'm sure. I can see my entire life unfolding in front of me and it's magnificent and Monika Sen will be remembered only for being a fucking thief people will loathe her and love me. Where the fuck is Pihu, she's not here yet, I can't ask for her advice but what the fuck does she know anyway, she's just a dumb teenager; all she's interested in is fucking Ranjit.

Living My Best Life

1 January 2021

Gyms, yoga studios and other fitness centres have always used the arrival of a new calendar year as a marketing opportunity to sell people the exciting possibility of a new body, new mind, new *you*. But it wasn't until the end of 2020 that such promotions caught Zeenat's attention. And once they did, she immediately became obsessed with the idea of fitness. In a matter of minutes, she had completed the process of downloading an app, filling in her information, setting her goals and signing up for a week-long free trial. The only problem was that she was now on the seventh day of the free trial without having done a single workout routine.

The previous year had been rough for a lot of people, for a lot of different reasons. For Zeenat, it had been especially difficult. She tried not to complain and reminded herself to check her privilege constantly. After all, everyone she loved was alive and safe, and she was healthy. At least, her body was.

She had only moved to America in the fall of 2019. It had been hard to move 7000 miles away from home to a foreign country, on her own for the first time in her life. But she had been determined from the beginning to make the most of her time there and go home having acquired an experience of a lifetime. It was this determination alone that kept her from turning around and taking the first flight back when she first came to realize, to her disappointment, that the city that was to be her home for the next two years, while she pursued a master's in English literature, was a full four-hour bus ride away from New York City. Although, technically, Binghamton is a city in New York state, it turned out to be quite a bit different from the New York she had expected when she had applied to her university. Those expectations were based primarily on movies, TV shows and entire songs dedicated to the greatest city in the world. No one ever wrote a song about Binghamton. And if they did, Zeenat would feel bad for them.

Her best friend from Delhi had moved to Manhattan a year before she landed. When Zeenat expressed her displeasure with her new home, her friend had promised her that they would see each other every other weekend, explore the museums, cultural sites, and all the restaurants and clubs in the city Zeenat's heart desired to eat or dance at. This way, Zeenat could still cling to her plan to experience the New York she had dreamt about.

A short seven months later, everyone was talking about the novel coronavirus. Her roommates, Mona and Sunny, didn't pay much attention to it, focusing instead on their classes and keeping their love affair secret from

Sunny's girlfriend. But Zeenat spent her nights obsessively scrolling through her social media accounts, absorbing all the information and misinformation served on her screens. *Doomscrolling*, Twitter called it.

Suddenly, the world around her changed. Zeenat had seen it coming, had even expected it. Even then, it failed to blunt the shock of the impact. Zeenat's life shrank to her small room in their small apartment, her phone and computer screens becoming the only windows to the world outside. When the world came to a standstill, all movements were shifted to the digital space. And, because screens were the only avenues with any movement, it was impossible to look away.

At first, Zeenat didn't think the lockdown would affect her too much personally. From the beginning, Zeenat recognized that she wasn't a victim of the pandemic, just a bystander. Yes, she was affected, but in a much smaller way, relatively. People were getting sick, dying, losing their loved ones, their livelihoods. Meanwhile, Zeenat was forced to stay home … and that was all. As sacrifices go, that wasn't a big ask. After all, she could still take her classes online, call her mom and text her friends.

Slowly, as the weather got warmer, the same small sacrifice began to seem bigger. She had arrived in Binghamton in August, had the chance to enjoy a few weeks of fall before it became progressively cold. When the temperature dropped below freezing and snow blanketed her city, Zeenat decided to put her exploration plans on hold till spring. The coronavirus arrived in New York before spring, and didn't leave when summer came, or fall, and soon, it was winter again.

Zeenat learned a lot in 2020. About pandemics, racial unrest, the economy, climate change, police brutality, American elections – all the things her screens fed to her every day. She learned to take a break, stay still, be okay with her loneliness. She held on, waiting for all of this to be over, for things to go back to normal.

She knew fully well that the world wasn't even close to normal, but there was the hope of a vaccine now. Zeenat dared to hope that the vaccine would put the world back on track towards reopening. So when, in the last week of 2020, an advertisement for a fitness app presented itself to her, Zeenat impulsively clicked on it.

She had never really considered fitness before. Health, sure. She ate nutritious, well-balanced meals in a routine way every day. She drank enough water and tried to get enough sleep. These measures had been enough in a pre-pandemic world, but nine months of stillness had left her feeling … soft. She had noticed roundness where there used to be angles, and had decided to join a six-week programme to get back in shape.

Not that she didn't accept her body the way it was, because she did. She had learned on Instagram that it was her responsibility to love herself, and treat her body and mind with kindness. So, she thanked her body for all that it did for her, showed her appreciation to her physical form and, in a healthy way, decided to embark on the path to self-improvement.

She simply wanted to be the best version of herself. She would buy the six-week fitness programme for herself as a New Year's gift. But before that, she had to test out the app to make sure it was the right one for her. It was important to find what worked for you, she had read somewhere. Similar to the Confucian philosophy – choose a job you love, and you will never have to work a day in your life. Zeenat wanted to make sure that her workouts felt more like a choice than a burden.

Which is why, now, on day seven, as she stared at her screen, she questioned if this workout app was right for her. Judging by the fact that she hadn't even attempted to try it yet, maybe it was not. Was she just making excuses? No, no, she wasn't, she convinced herself.

Only a few hours remained before the free trial expired; it seemed unlikely that she would be following through with her plan.

Oh well, she thought to herself. The journey to becoming the best version of yourself and living your best life didn't have to start on the first of January. Calendars are a social construct anyway.

6 January 2021

Standing up for herself and speaking up more was also on Zeenat's self-improvement list. Growing up as a middle child in the small town of Ajmer, with parents who worked full-time as doctors, it had been easy for Zeenat to stay in her comfort zone: quiet, observant and happy. She never needed to step out of it, explore new avenues.

Before she moved to the US, her younger sister had told her, quite sternly, to try to make friends with Americans and other international students, as opposed to sticking with a closed Indians-only group and returning home with an incomplete educational experience. Zeenat had intended to follow her sister's advice; however, once she had arrived in Binghamton, she had found a room with Mona and Sunny within a week, and been introduced to their friends. In class, she'd sat next to Prateek, and then become friends with his friends. Without trying, she had found herself within a bubble of exclusively Indian friends, at home and school.

It was comfortable, familiar and fun. What did her younger sister know anyway? When you're in a foreign land, it's only normal to gravitate towards people who made you feel at home. She didn't like that their group referred to Americans as '*ye log*' (these people) or that they used Hindi to talk about others behind their back, only, they did so *in front* of them. It made Zeenat uncomfortable, but, besides those minor grievances, she liked her group of friends.

Well, everyone except Priyanka. For reasons Zeenat couldn't discern, Priyanka seemed to have chosen to criticize her every move. Zeenat had a lifelong experience of staying within the lines, so the fact that her every action was now able to entice outrage and ridicule in someone was unchartered waters for her.

It had started with small jibes like, 'Oh, you're wearing that T-shirt again?' which gradually built its way up to more personal things. Priyanka questioned why Zeenat never shared photos on Instagram. And why Zeenat still talked to her boyfriend back in India, instead of putting an end to the misery of a long-distance relationship and finding someone new in the US. After the first few months of the coronavirus lockdowns, when the restrictions had been somewhat lifted, Priyanka was constantly curious about why Zeenat chose to avoid joining them for their backyard barbeques and game nights.

'What are you afraid of? We don't have COVID. And even if we did, even if you got it somehow, you'll live!'

'I just want everyone to be safe,' Zeenat would say to defend herself.

'Come on! Don't be such a buzzkill.'

Zeenat was proud of herself for not giving in to peer pressure. Even though she hadn't said all the things she wanted to say to Priyanka, she had stood up for herself in a small way and done only what she was comfortable with.

In an ideal world, Zeenat would've gathered the courage to show Priyanka the graphs with the rising numbers, news about small businesses shutting down, people dying, healthcare workers begging and pleading everyone to stay home. Just because the government wasn't enforcing a lockdown any longer didn't mean people couldn't still use their better judgement and keep everyone safe. Instead, Zeenat simply muted Priyanka's Instagram account, in order to avoid seeing her break all precautions and live it up in a pandemic.

One day, Zeenat would stand up to Priyanka. But for now, she was focusing on her own mental health while still maintaining COVID safety. She ensured that she went for a twenty-minute walk every day, no matter how cold the weather. It energized her, sustained her motivation to get up in the morning.

This particular morning, she had decided to go to a Starbucks to get herself some coffee. She wasn't much of a coffee drinker; fully aware of her obsessive tendencies, she made sure to stay away from caffeine to avoid an addiction. But every once in a while, she would treat herself to an almond milk latte.

'Thank you,' Zeenat said through her mask, picking up her cup from the counter.

It wasn't until she was outside and had lowered her mask for a sip that she realized that the barista had used cow milk instead. This was a problem not only because Zeenat was trying to avoid animal products as much as possible, for the environment, but also because she had developed an intolerance to lactose upon moving to the US and consuming growth hormone–infused dairy. Maybe not a complete intolerance, but definitely a sensitivity.

She contemplated her options. She had already taken a sip. Maybe she hadn't spoken clearly enough? Placing orders at Starbucks was always so stressful. Maybe it wasn't the barista's fault. She couldn't possibly confront him when she wasn't sure. But she also couldn't drink dairy without risking diarrhoea. Wasn't there another Starbucks close by? She pulled out her phone with freezing-cold fingers to check how far she would have to walk to get the right order of coffee.

No, a voice inside her jolted her. *You know fully well that you placed the right order. You practised it on your walk over.*

She had. She knew she had placed the right order, making sure to speak very clearly.

Don't be a pushover. How would you ever stand up to Priyanka, your friend, if you can't even stand up for yourself to a stranger?

She knew what she had to do. It took Zeenat a few moments, but eventually, she did put one foot in front of the other and walk back into the Starbucks.

🌹

18 January 2021

In the first two weeks of January, Zeenat's life hadn't transformed quite as much as she had anticipated. 2021 wasn't very different from 2020. Her big plans for fitness had failed so far. She ended up buying the app, after the trial ended, but hadn't even started the six-week programme yet. All she had managed to do were two twenty-minute sessions of Pilates. That wasn't nothing, she told herself now. At least she wasn't completely inactive like she had been in 2020. Even if she kept up this low-intensity, infrequent schedule of once a week, by the end of the year, she would still have done fifty-two more workouts than she did the year before that.

In any case, fitness was a marathon, not a sprint. Even if she did manage to do six weeks of six high-intensity workouts a week, it didn't mean she would never have to exercise again for the rest of her life. Of course not. She had to find something that she didn't only love but could also sustain. Pilates wasn't it. She might try yoga next.

This internal monologue made Zeenat feel better and she moved on to the next big health-related self-improvement goal she wanted to work on: nutrition.

Zeenat was trying to switch to a vegan diet. It started when she developed a sensitivity to lactose and began researching alternatives. That opened the floodgates to the evils of the American dairy industry and its environmental impact, which in turn led her to a research conducted by the University of Oxford, asserting that cutting meat and dairy products from their diet could reduce a person's carbon footprint by up to 73 per cent. Upon further inquiry, Zeenat found that a vegan diet was considered to be the 'single biggest way' to reduce one's environmental impact on earth. It conserved water, kept the soil and air clean, reduced energy consumption, and, if done right, could be more nutritious for the body overall.

In the past, Zeenat had dismissed veganism on the basis of misinformation and prejudice. Vegans were often made fun of, considered snowflakes and seen as people who thought they were superior to everyone else, people who judged others for consuming meat. But the more she read, the more Zeenat realized that the foundation of veganism was quite strong, its arguments quite valid.

These arguments made her change her diet setting on her fitness app. Now, she was determined to cook nutritious, vegan meals for one month, to start with. She had been successful too, though it hadn't exactly been easy, with Sunny cooking butter chicken in the kitchen while she chopped vegetables for pav bhaji.

'Are you seriously not going to eat with us today too?' Mona asked. She sat perched on the counter, looking down into the pot of chicken.

'I'll eat with you ... but not what you are having.' Zeenat shrugged, chuckling. Veganism seemed like such an important step in the right direction in her own head, but whenever someone else talked about it, Zeenat felt as though what she was doing was so silly.

'Dude, you're missing out,' Sunny said teasingly.

'Don't tempt me! If I'm going to make it, I need your support!'

'And our support you shall receive,' Mona said. She took the ladle from Sunny, ran her finger over it, and licked it clean. 'Too bad this is so delicious. *Ghar ki yaad aa gayi, yaar.* It has made me homesick.'

'You're bad.' Zeenat shook her head and looked away, and mumbled under her breath, 'Fourteen days to go.'

'And then what? You'll go on a meat rampage?' Sunny asked.

'Not exactly, not meat. I'll eat seafood once a week and poultry once a month.'

'That's not too bad, actually,' Mona said thoughtfully. 'You can eat salmon and tuna and chicken. Even turkey. Just not pork or lamb or goat or beef?'

'That's the plan. I don't think I'll miss meat; I didn't ever eat pork or beef anyway,' Zeenat said. 'It's just chicken that's hard to resist … but I want to slowly phase it out and stick to a pescatarian diet.'

'Hats off, man. I could never do that,' Mona said, jumping off the counter. 'Just the thought of living without Sunny's famous Punjabi butter chicken makes me want to cry.'

'If it makes you feel any better, I'm fighting away tears right now just smelling Sunny's famous Punjabi butter chicken,' Zeenat said. She laughed to mask the sincerity of her admission.

'What's the verdict on eggs?' Sunny asked.

'Haven't read up about it. From what I know, there are farm-raised, cage-free options, but I'm not sure how much of that is just greenwashing … There's a lot of reading to do …'

As they chatted away, Zeenat felt stronger in her resolve. The fact that she had witnesses definitely helped her stick with her plan. So, when they finished cooking their separate lunches, they sat down at the kitchen counter together to eat. Zeenat might have failed in her fitness goals and plans to stand up to Priyanka, but at least she was succeeding in going vegan for a month. Minus that accidental sip of cow-milk coffee, but she had made sure to get that problem rectified. All in all, she wouldn't say her New Year resolutions were going too poorly. She cherished the small sense of accomplishment she felt.

25 January 2021

Switching to a vegan diet was where Zeenat's advocacy for the planet had started, but it certainly couldn't end there. The year 2020 had opened her eyes to many new issues, one of which was the impact of the fast-fashion industry on the environment. As she read more about it, she found out extensive information about unethical business practices, low wages and even slave labour, child labour and sweatshops. After many horrifying hours reading about the fashion industry, it was clear to Zeenat that she couldn't support fast fashion any longer, something she had done mindlessly for several years.

According to the United Nations, the fashion industry was the second-largest polluter of clean water, responsible for 10 per cent of global greenhouse gas emissions, and consumed more energy than aviation and shipping combined. On top of that, every second of every day, one trash-truck worth of textiles was either burned or sent to a landfill. The data was overwhelming. Zeenat couldn't even look at her closet without feeling overwhelmed with guilt. She didn't need all these clothes she owned. She hadn't even worn half of them more than a handful of times.

Donating wasn't a good option either, she had learned. Most, about 85 per cent, of the donated clothes ended up in a landfill or was burned, and out of the 15 per cent that did go to second-hand shops, only a small percentage was bought. It could take over 200 years for the materials to decompose in a landfill. Not to mention the methane gas generated during the decomposition process, and toxic chemicals and dyes that leached into the groundwater and soil.

Zeenat felt increasingly helpless. She looked into recycling, repurposing, swapping and thrifting. She thought about her mother, who never threw out anything. She always found a reuse potential for everything: old T-shirts as cleaning rags, old towels as mops, jam jars to store spices. She believed in caring for things, and when they broke, she made sure to mend them. When she and her siblings outgrew their clothes, or simply got tired of them, her mother would always find specific people to hand them down to, making sure each article of clothing would be used by someone. Nothing was thrown away unless it became completely useless. These weren't new concepts. These basics of minimal living had come naturally to her mother. Now, Zeenat tried her best to bring them into her lifestyle.

After much researching, Zeenat made a to-do list of different ways to reduce her impact and, in the end, reached a conclusion: the best thing she could do was to stop buying clothes. A less drastic option was to ask herself every time she wanted to buy something: will I wear this at least thirty times? Another was to buy only from ethical and sustainable brands, but those cost a lot more than fast fashion. Yet another was to swap clothes with friends, or buy from thrift stores, since used clothes consumed no new energy or labour to produce. Renting was an option too. Choosing quality over quantity, repairing clothes or altering them so they fit better, buying more mindfully were all good options as well. But, in the end, not buying anything at all seemed like the best and simplest alternative. It was also the hardest.

The thing about the pandemic was that even though it shut everything down and limited everyone to their homes, it also created a burning desire for newness and action in people. Every time Zeenat turned to her screens, consumerism was shoved into her face. Every day, she woke up and checked her Instagram. Every day she saw people in new clothes, shoes, jewellery and make-up, carrying new handbags and drinks with plastic straws. She was served targeted ads for the brands she used to shop for, before she started the no-buy for the month of January. And once she clicked on one of the ads, they reappeared with doubled ferocity over her next visits to the app.

Every time she went online, there was temptation. She struggled to keep it under control. So, she set guidelines for herself to help her walk away without giving in to impulse buying. She wrote them down on Post-it notes and stuck them on the wall in her room, above her desk.

- Visualize the money you would've spent on shopping in your bank account.
- Imagine what else that money could buy.
- Walk through what would happen when the package arrives: you'll open it, try it on, fold it, put it away, throw out the packaging (landfill!!!)
- Sunny and Mona will judge you and make jokes about packages arriving every day.
- Where are you even going? You don't need clothes.
- Try the five-second rule. Simply click away within five seconds.

The reason she had to take this so seriously and make this elaborate system to keep her on track was that it was far too easy to slip up. A mix of these guidelines had helped her not buy anything for twenty-four days so far. Of course, she was allowed to buy groceries and hygiene products, but only when she ran out of them and needed to repurchase. The keyword was *need*, not *want*.

It was on day twenty-five that Anthropologie presented her with a '50% off sale items' ad. That meant that the sweater she liked, originally priced at $100, and discounted to $50, was now available for just $25. That was a steal. And it wasn't something frivolous. She needed a sweater. Hello, she lived in upstate New York, where it was freezing cold eight months of the year. Also, she definitely was going to wear it more than thirty times. Sure, she wasn't supposed to buy anything for seven more days, but who knew how long the sale would last? What was the point of risking paying twice the amount of what she had would have to pay now, just to follow a stupid no-buy she made up for herself? It didn't make any sense. It made no difference whatsoever on the environment whether she bought the sweater today or one week from now.

So, she chided herself for making up silly rules, and placed the sweater in her cart. Shipping was $7. Free if her order was $50 or more. Which meant that she needed to spend $25 more to save $7 on shipping. If you think about it, that meant she would essentially be paying $18 for something that was worth $25, which would probably already be down from $100. If you think about it, she would lose money by *not* buying something now, when it was on sale. That logic made sense in her head, so she clicked on the SALE tab to search for something else she could buy to qualify for free shipping.

Her Post-it notes stared at her from the wall in front of her. Zeenat kept her eyes trained on her computer screen. She was being too harsh on herself. She deserved something nice. She shouldn't feel guilty for treating herself every once in a while. She had successfully completed twenty-five days of the no-buy. One small purchase didn't matter. No matter how strongly she felt, the Post-its stared down at her as she scrolled through the sale section.

🌹

31 January 2021

Last day of the month. Zeenat wanted to make it count, while also recognizing that she shouldn't put too much undue pressure on herself and prioritize her mental health over all else. Keeping that in mind, she thought back to her mental list of goals and their results.

1. **Fitness: FAIL**
   Her fitness goal had reduced from an intense six-week HIIT programme to one Pilates class a week. That meant she was doing one low-intensity workout per week, instead of six high-intensity sessions. Strangely, she was okay with it. By the fourth week, she was able to complete moves she hadn't been able to perform at first. That was progress. So fitness felt like a win, even though she had failed to achieve what she had set out to do.

2. **Veganuary: WIN**
   Zeenat had excelled at maintaining a vegan diet throughout January, hence establishing a good foundation for the year. This transition was going according to plan. Zeenat took a moment to appreciate her efforts and take pride in the results, just like the article she had read online said to do.

3. **No-buy: FAIL**
   She had failed the no-buy challenge and ended up spending $77 at an unethical, unsustainable brand to buy a sweater she was convinced she needed and a dress she had no occasion to wear. When the package arrived, she had quickly, shamefully, removed the tags and thrown away the packaging. Now, these new pieces of clothing sat in

her closet, indistinguishable from the old ones. Ultimately, that slip in willpower didn't feel worth it to Zeenat.

4. **Speaking up: FAIL**
At most, her goal to stand up for herself had seen partial success. While she hadn't confronted Priyanka, which was what the actual goal was, she had spoken up at Starbucks and gotten her coffee order corrected.

Zeenat was unhappy with the 25 per cent success rate. She still had an opportunity to flip that last fail into a win, because Priyanka had texted Zeenat to ask her to go for a walk. Fifty per cent sounded far better than 25 per cent. She could live with 50 per cent.

In the past, Zeenat had only spent time with Priyanka in a group setting. So, when Priyanka asked Zeenat to meet her alone, the request made Zeenat a little anxious. She shrugged it away as she picked up her new sweater from the top of the pile of clothes in her closet and put it on. See, she was already putting it to use.

To prepare herself for the confrontation, Zeenat read articles titled '6 Ways to Cut a Toxic Friend Out of Your Life for Good' and 'How to Gracefully End a Toxic Friendship'. She was ready. If Priyanka so much as made a snide remark about Zeenat's social media absence or dark circles, Zeenat was prepared to put an end to such bullying then and there.

By the time she left her apartment, Zeenat was almost shaking with anticipation and dread. *No*, she told herself, as she walked to the park where they were meeting. *You won't back out.*

She spotted Priyanka waving at her from the other side of the street. She crossed over when the light turned and walked towards Zeenat.

Priyanka stopped six feet away from Zeenat and said, 'How's it going?'

Right away, Zeenat sensed it. Her voice was different. Her whole demeanour had changed. She looked nothing like her lively Instagram selfies – the structured leather coat was replaced by a warm-looking puffer jacket, and her beanie hat was pulled down to cover her ears completely, hiding all her hair, even her sideburns, making her head look like an egg. Zeenat had never seen Priyanka use her beanie for warmth before. Something was wrong.

'What's wrong?' she asked, lowering her mask, since Priyanka was honouring the six-feet rule and they were outdoors.

Priyanka lowered her mask on cue. No make-up. Something was definitely wrong. 'Mm, nothing,' she said, walking on the snow. 'Just quarantine blues, I guess.'

'Quarantine's been going on for almost a year now. What changed?' Zeenat walked next to her.

'That. That it's been so long. We'll graduate in a few months, and it's all over. Our very expensive American experience wasted in a lockdown. Massive student loans, no jobs on the horizon, a dead economy and a messed-up immigration system.'

Zeenat felt guilty about not having student loans; she had received a full scholarship based on merit. Additionally, it had always been her plan to go back home after finishing her master's anyway, and she had never been delusional enough to believe that she would have lucrative career opportunities with her MA in English literature. She wanted to go back home and teach at a university, while working on her PhD. So, none of the very real problems Priyanka had listed applied to Zeenat.

'Yeah, it's all looking pretty bleak,' she said nonetheless. 'It'll be okay though, eventually. It won't be like this forever.'

'Yeah … you don't know that.' Priyanka's shoulders drooped further.

I'm just trying to stay optimistic, Zeenat wanted to snap. *There's nothing wrong with that. As long as it's not toxic positivity.* But Priyanka's tone hadn't been snide. It had just been sad. So Zeenat stopped herself and instead said, 'You're right, I *don't* know that. I just say that to myself to get through the day.'

'Right?' Priyanka said passionately, as if a switch had flipped inside her. 'I keep having these talks with myself every day, every hour actually. Like I'm my own therapist, and need to keep myself on track. It's like I'm in a constant state of crisis and I'm the only person who can help me. It's terrifying. One moment, I'm fine. The next, boom, existential crisis. I'm just so sick and tired of being alone all the time, with my sad thoughts. I'm not a sad person. I have no interest in being sad … But how do I stop? I can't. It's just who I am now …'

As Priyanka spoke, Zeenat walked by her side, six feet apart, and watched her. For the first time, she was seeing the person behind the beautiful, strong and sometimes bratty demeanour. At the end of the day, Priyanka was just a person. Albeit quite rude and intrusive at times, but she wasn't exactly the villain Zeenat had built her up to be. Maybe Priyanka criticized things about Zeenat that she didn't like in herself. That's something that happens. Maybe she set standards for Zeenat that she had for herself. It was wrong to do so, but maybe she couldn't help it. Maybe it came from a place of insecurity. Or maybe she was just mean. Yet, that didn't affect Zeenat quite as much, after seeing Priyanka be this vulnerable, this human, for a moment.

The more Priyanka opened up about her internal struggles, the more it became clear to Zeenat that she didn't need to be confronted, at least not today. She just needed to be heard. Today, Zeenat's job was to not add to Priyanka's problems. She needed to be a good friend, to listen.

Zeenat was going to mark 'speaking up' as a WIN anyway. She wasn't delusional enough to think that this was the beginning of an amazing new friendship. She was probably not going to be close friends with Priyanka in the future. They just didn't connect that way. But, for now, at least she could be there for her in her time of need, and be unbothered and unaffected by her. And that counted as a win.

Guru

Dear Amit Sir,

You must be just as surprised to be reading this as I am to be writing this to you. It has been thirteen years since you were my teacher, ten years since we last spoke, and yet, when I think about death, I am terrified of not having said this to you before my time on this planet is up. I apologize. What a grim way to start this letter. Unfortunately, it has taken the literal thought of dying to jolt me into action and tell you some things I've been meaning to share with you for over a decade.

Growing up, the word 'guru' was considered to have divine significance, a term used to mirror the respect our society showed our teachers. It doesn't retain the same meaning now. The term 'guru' has been bastardized, adopted by other languages, cultures, and turned into a buzzword to be used generously and applied to a variety of situations. It's a dirty word now.

Twenty years ago, when I was a kid, we were told that all our schoolteachers were our gurus. I could never surrender to that logic. Even as a nine year old, I recognized that the lady who taught us maths for forty-five minutes every day was doing so in exchange for a salary, not out of the selfless goodness of her heart. Not that she didn't deserve the money for the work that she was doing. I would argue that, in fact, she deserved quite a bit more than she was making at that school, but it was the over-idealization of people who chose to teach as a career that bothered me. Most teachers I've had didn't, through their actions, demand that all-encompassing, indisputable sort of respect. The respect we had to bestow upon them was mandatory.

Thirteen years ago, when I joined the school where you taught chemistry, not much had changed in my views about putting teachers on a pedestal. In fact, in my two years at that school, I lost respect for most of the teachers there because of the way they treated me. At the time, I believed that I deserved that treatment. Anyone who didn't get high scores in tests and wasn't the perfect, studious student deserved to be berated by teachers – that lesson had been ingrained in me since childhood. But as I've thought about these teachers over the years, as an adult, I feel for the sixteen-year-old me who came to your school. She didn't do anything to deserve such malice.

I'll give you some examples:

1.   Patil Sir: The biology teacher who openly hated me. If I had to guess why, it was probably because I have always been bad at surrendered listening. So, while I wasn't an especially wild child, I did question things. That might have proved challenging for him. Let me tell you about two instances:

Once, he refused to accept my project because I referred to a book other than the one he personally preferred. I asked him to provide me a written letter, so that I could show it to my parents when they asked why I got a zero on the project.

Another time, he told me and my classmate Rupa that we would never become doctors. There were only four students in his class (the rest of my section had opted for maths) and he went as far as wagering that he would give us both ₹10,000 if either of us ever got into medical school. What kind of teacher bets on their students' failure? I believe Rupa did end up becoming a doctor, but Patil Sir did succeed in sucking out all my passion for biology in the two years that I spent in his class.

2.   KD Sir: The maths teacher, who I had almost no relationship with, because I wasn't in his class and we almost never interacted. I still remember the time when he motioned me with his fingers to approach him. I looked around to make sure I was

the person he was pointing to, before going over. He handed me the briefcase he was holding, and asked me to put it in his office, which was about a mere ten steps behind him. I did so, and came back to him, expecting to find out the reason he had summoned me over, now that we had the briefcase out of the way. He paused his conversation with Patil Sir to stare at me like I was stupid, annoyed at me for interrupting him. That's when I realized that it was some kind of twisted powerplay. He was treating me like his butler, just because he could. I walked away, feeling small and ashamed. I have never forgotten that moment. *He did that just because he could.* That thought has never fully left me.

3.   Usha Ma'am: The economics teacher, who, again, I didn't have much to do with, because I wasn't in her class either. She ran an informal private club of sorts. It was a closed group of cool girls from the economics and science sections, huddled together, laughing at private jokes. The teacher and the students in that group had all been at that school since it first opened, a few years before I joined. The group was impenetrable. I know I shouldn't have cared for their approval or validation, but I did. They excluded me from the beginning and my petty little heart was hurt. The only time Usha Ma'am talked to me was to ask what kind of moisturizer I used for my face. I was surprised at the question. She

explained that she meant it as a compliment and was looking for tips for oily skin which was prone to pimples. I told her the truth, which was that I used my mother's Vaseline body lotion on my arms and face. She laughed, and jokingly announced to all the girls around that she was jealous of my skin type, which was perfect despite the body lotion, whereas she spent so much money on cosmetics for her skin. I was embarrassed that we didn't have enough money to buy a moisturizer meant specifically for the face.

4.   A junior teacher whose name I can't remember: She sent word through a student that she was looking for me, and when I found her, she asked me what was going on between Pratham and me. I told her the truth, that there was nothing between us, but she didn't believe me. Soon after that, there were rumours about Pratham and me circulating in school. It was the strangest thing, because as you know, I was in a relationship with another student.

And clearly, thirteen years later, when I look back at the two years I went to that school, these memories still jump out to me, so they must've had an impact on me. The only reason I'm bringing up these incidents (other than the fact that they surfaced to my mind uninvited as soon as I thought back to my two years at that school) is to show you how starkly different your treatment of me was, compared to the other teachers. And exactly how much I needed it then, and how much it matters to me even now.

The smallest things can have the biggest impact. We can never know how the most insignificant thing we say or do can affect someone else. We can say the smallest thing and forget it, but that small thing can ruin someone's life, or it can completely change the way they see themselves. I want to make sure you know that your small acts of kindness held me together for a long time.

The only two teachers who went beyond the scope of their jobs, that of teaching a specific subject, and actually mentored students and helped us navigate our last two years in school were you and Kapila Ma'am. As far as Kapila Ma'am is concerned, I can see why she liked me. I always scored high, if not the highest in class, in English. So, the English teacher liked me.

But I never did well in chemistry. So, what did you see in me? I still don't know what it was, but I know that I needed it. To an extent, it instilled confidence in me. A confidence in myself, when everyone else made me feel worthless. In those two years, all I wanted was to finish school and leave as soon as possible. You made my time there bearable.

As a teenager, there wasn't much I had control over. I felt helpless, inconsequential. The hierarchy of our Indian school system is such that if you don't excel in exams, you are essentially a lesser being. You are treated in an inferior way, and that was exactly my experience all through school. Yet, you maintained that I had potential. You were vocal about it. You told me that, more than once. You told other students, teachers, my parents. It's unlikely that you changed the way they saw me, but you certainly changed the way *I* saw me.

In the end, nothing anyone else thought mattered. The only thing that mattered was that I believed in myself, and that plant of self-belief is a result of the seedling of confidence you planted in my mind.

I also really appreciate, even to this day, that you never gave me any special treatment, or free passes, no matter how much you believed in me. In eleventh class, I failed the chemistry final exam by just a few marks. You didn't just give me those marks to gently tug me over to the other side. No, I studied for a month and took the supplement exam. While all my friends started the twelfth class, I had to wait, study, take the test and pass chemistry before joining them. I didn't score well – I was distracted by my boyfriend at the time – but I passed. I still remember sitting in the large classroom in a wing of the school I rarely frequented, taking the test with two other kids, both of whom were even lower in the food chain than I was. I was ashamed. I had never failed a subject in the final exams.

Thinking back now, it's not much more than a funny story to tell my friends: that I was hopeless at chemistry but still somehow ended up going to college for a bachelor's in pharmacy. Back then, it was embarrassing, yet it never diminished my respect for you. On the contrary, that was exactly what I needed. To learn that good results had to be earned. There are no handouts in the game of life. In the years after school, I have faced many challenges. I have struggled through them, and I have fought to make my way to the other side. I knew how.

I'm sure you heard that I ended up doing a bachelor's in pharmacy. Once again, organic chemistry became the bane of my existence. But this time, I was patient with it and, to my surprise, once I began to understand the fundamentals, everything else became so clear. I got good at it. I used to think about you a lot during those years in college.

I wanted to reach out to you, but I couldn't. I don't want to make excuses; I accept that the blame lies fully with me. When my sister died, it became hard for me to be around people who knew both of us. You knew her, you taught her. She was smart in an obvious sort of way. Teachers, including you, loved her. It didn't hurt that she was fun and lovable, whereas I was pretty quiet, and quite mediocre at everything. A student without much of a perceivable ambition.

Just because it wasn't obviously present didn't mean that I wasn't ambitious. In fact, I was secretly very ambitious. But ambition without work to back it turns into anxiety. I wanted to do … something. Be a part of something bigger than myself. But I didn't have direction. I could see no paths in front of me to pursue. The ambition turned into anxiety inside me, that anxiety ate at my self-confidence. Soon, I was nothing. No one.

The self-doubt was crippling. We all grow up thinking that we're special. We have a small voice in our heads telling us that we are going to go on to do great things. For me, that voice wasn't just mine. It was yours too. But without direction, I felt hopeless. I wasn't in charge. My anxiety got the better of me, which is why, after school ended, I started college to pursue pharmacy, believing that I wasn't good enough, determined enough, dedicated enough, to study for the medical entrance exams.

My first year in college was a blur of new friends, distractions and anxiety caused by the anticipation of a mediocre life that waited for me, due to my inaction. I was going to have an ordinary life, because I didn't do anything to put me on track for an extraordinary one.

In my second year in college, I turned away, inwards. I tried, consciously, to think of a way out. What could I do? How could I try to reach this *potential* you talked about, that I secretly knew I had? I turned to books. First, I read a lot. The part of me that always seems to *know* things knew that I would one day write a book. It was when I read a terrible book that I realized that that day had arrived.

Before stumbling upon this terrible book, I had had the good fortune of only reading great books from my father's library. This particular book was a gift from a friend. And it changed my life. For the first time in my life, I saw a published, successful book be so grotesque. And if that kind of writing could be published and adored, I knew I could write far better.

That was when I wrote my first book. I had finally found direction, halfway through college.

Before I could call you, my life changed once again. My sister died two days before my book released. My mother told me later that she had been planning a surprise celebration for the launch of my book. I have written over a dozen books since then. I've never celebrated the launch of any of them.

It's still hard for me to be around people who knew her. I have put her memories in a box. The seventeen years of her life are tucked away in a corner of my heart. It haunts me, keeps me from communicating with the people I love. I still talk to people who knew us, but communicating in any meaningful way, exposing covered wounds, is difficult. This is why I write romance novels about fictional characters – so that I don't have to write about myself. This is why my social media offers little information about how I'm really feeling or things I really care about. It's to protect myself.

But I'm working on it. I'm working on myself.

I vaguely remember, as I write this, that our paths crossed once, a few years after school. That you told me you were proud of me. Or maybe it was just wishful thinking. For someone who remembers everything, it frustrates me that I'm hazy on this. In any case, just to be safe, I'm writing this to you.

To tell you that you affected my life in a positive way. To thank you for planting that encouraging voice in my head. To reinforce that you have significantly impacted the way I see myself.

We live our lives as though we would all live till we're old and die of natural causes. We don't think about death enough. I used to think about death a lot, in a disturbing, grim way. Now, from time to time, I make it a point to do it intentionally, think about why I'm on this planet, what I'm doing, what I still have to do before my time is up.

This letter is one such thing. I wanted to write this to you.

I don't know where you are now, but I know that I'll find you, and I'll send you a copy of this book. I will bookmark this letter, so that I can finally communicate with you in a way I have been meaning to for a long time.

I know we will talk again soon. But, for now, please accept this as my small token of gratitude. By helping me trust myself, you saved me.

Thank you,
Nikita

Mirror Mirror

In the mirror, Sher sees a man with a head full of memories. He sees Leo and baby Preet; their laughter rings in his ears. He sees a proud father. He sees a man who is living in the present, taking care of his mind and body in order to have his second innings in life, before he's reunited with the love of his life.

Tutu inspects his reflection in the long mirror attached to the Godrej almirah in Bua's room. His biceps are growing, he's sure of it. He has been lifting the empty water bottle filled with sand that Nishu Bhaiya made for him every morning and night. Forty curls every day. He is already the strongest boy in his class. Soon, he will be the strongest superhero on planet earth. Maybe he'll even train Popo to become his sidekick.

When Falguni looks in the mirror, she sees Natasha, a woman who had been through immense trauma in her past and had a long road of recovery ahead of her. She sees someone who, through truth, finally let her guard down and asked for help. Next to her in the mirror is Gautam, who doesn't fully understand the extent of her devastation, but stands by her regardless. They live in her truth.

Avani sees someone who can't stop lying. To others, and to herself. She sees a woman who finds red flag after red flag right in front of her, and turns away. She looks to her right, at Ravi's reflection. He loves her, she tells herself, in his own way, to the extent that he is capable. Next to her, Ravi sees himself in the mirror. He turns to inspect every angle of his face, making notes of what his best features are, and what to post on social media.

Raveena looks long and hard in the mirror. She feels a certain calm sweep over her, as she looks into her own eyes. The conversation with the stranger on the plane has sparked some conversations between her and Atul. While she found beauty in the 'tending to the plant of your love' analogy, Atul had felt his heart sink. Many long nights of grueling conversations later, they come to the realization that her initial gut feeling was in fact, true. Their relationship has run its course. A dead plant cannot be revived. Raveena is in the eye of the storm now, but she knows she will come out of it stronger.

Prakash doesn't look in the mirror. He cradles his grandchild gently in his arms, and peers into the small, pinched face of the most beautiful baby in the world, blooming in front of his eyes like a vibrant flower.

Tears blur Barkha's vision. Talha slides his arm around her from behind, holding her up. Barkha looks at his husband in the mirror. Then she looks at herself – a mother, but no longer a sister.

Gauri sees determination in her eyes, determination to destroy her plagiarist, Monika Sen. Zeenat sees an imperfect person in the mirror. But she also sees someone who tries, and can learn to be less hard on herself.

When I look in the mirror, I see a person who dreams.

Acknowledgements

In 2020, I had my fair share of mental breakdowns. In 2021, I put pen to paper (and fingers to keyboard) and wrote this book. The writing part didn't require much assistance from others, but I needed plenty of help just to get to the point where I could write. What a wonderful opportunity this is for me to be able to express my gratitude here.

My parents, for making me the person I am. Your strength, resilience and generosity have set a precedent for me that I can only aspire to. My brother, and little cousins, Tutu and Popo, for providing comedic relief and keeping said parents entertained while I'm locked down 12,000 kilometres away from home. I hope to see you very soon.

Nick, I have never leaned on anyone quite as much as I have on you in the past year. Not just emotionally, but also in brainstorming story ideas, coming up with silly endings that don't make any sense and in providing feedback that I immediately shoot down, and then reconsider later, once I have had a chance to think. I have also thoroughly enjoyed horrifying you with crazy twists and turns from time to time. You're welcome.

My dear friends who only existed as faces on my phone screen or voices in my ear this year. I can't wait to squeeze you soon. Hina, for being the sweetest friend to me, and also for all your help in running Nikita's Bookshelf. Nejla, for always hearing me and responding to my full-page text messages with two pages. Ritu, for having the same crises as me, so we can be in the worst of it together. Sandra and Yannick, for bringing the sweetest little baby Noah into this world. Laura, Scott and baby Joaquín for giving me so much faith and optimism. Cynthia, for your unwavering support and laughter.

The pandemic arrived a few short months after I moved to Montréal. I'm so grateful to have found a handful of amazing new people here before everything shut down. Thank you, Melanié, for being by my side, every single time I needed perspective and sanity, and for making fun of me for pronouncing French words incorrectly. Steph, for your kind heart, and for making vegan recipes and sangria with me. Elena, for letting me impart my very limited Sephora and Mario Kart wisdom on to you. Ava, for the walks, picnics by the canal, and for being a safe place to complain.

And of course, my extraordinary team that made this book possible. My agent, Anish Chandy, for your invaluable insight and honesty. Shabnam Srivastava, for your enthusiasm and our hilarious exchanges. My editor, Swati Daftuar, for your astute observations and invaluable contribution to these stories. Paloma Dutta and everyone in the editorial team, for your immaculate attention to detail. Bonita Shimray and the design team for this beautiful cover.

Diya Kar, for believing in the concept of this book from the beginning. Ananth Padmanabhan, for seeing me, and also being in my corner.

To you, my readers, for your patience and acceptance. Special shout-out to the terrific members of Nikita's Bookshelf. Our book club is a community that has kept so many of us afloat through so much. Can't wait to see you next month.

About the Author

Nikita Singh is the bestselling author of twelve books, including *The Reason Is You, Every Time It Rains* and *Like a Love Song*. She is also the editor of the collections of short stories *25 Strokes of Kindness and The Turning Point*.

After working in the book publishing industry in New Delhi for several years, she got her MFA in Creative Writing (Fiction) at The New School in New York. Invested in the fight against climate change, she works as the director of marketing of a solar energy company based in Brooklyn.

Nikita lives in Montréal, and runs a virtual book club called Nikita's Bookshelf. You can follow her on Instagram and Twitter (@singh_nikita) or visit nikitasbooks.com to learn more.

ALSO BY NIKITA SINGH

Love is a many-flavoured thing: it can go from vanilla to rainbow sprinkles in the blink of an eye. Four years ago, Maahis heart was broken into so many pieces that it looked like she might never put it back together again. Yet time has healed her wounds, and she has found her true calling – and even a dash or romance. But when the past comes knocking on her door, threatening to shatter a life she has carefully rebuilt, her world is turned upside-down. What will Maahi do when she is torn between her head and her heart? Emotionally charged and vivid, *Like a Love Song* is about the sort of love that consumes and sears you ... and the healing powers of true passion, threatening to shatter a life she has carefully rebuilt, her world is turned upside-down. What will Maahi do when she is torn between her head and her heart?

NIKITA SINGH

Every Time It Rains

Love is a dangerous thing. It brings with it great joy, and opens you up to pain. But does one really have the courage to say no and look the other way?

Laila is yet to recover from her painful past. Hurt, and untrusting of love, she is fully immersed in work, her only source of cheer. Her bakery franchise is very popular and she just might be able to go national, if she can pull off that big deal.

Just when things are looking up, along comes JD, an impetuous, free-spirited creature to stir up the calm. He's her exact opposite. Laila's self-destructive, he's life-affirming. She's cautious, he's buoyant. But here's the thing: he makes her feel the very things she wanted to forget. Stirring a familiar passion she longed for but had lost the courage to pursue. They are irrepressibly drawn to each other but will she ever be able to trust him?

Every Time It Rains is the story of every girl who has ever had her heart broken. And fallen in love again.

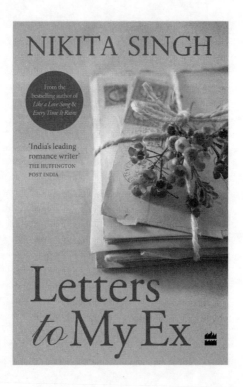

'It feels like I'm on autopilot; I have no control over anything. The pain of losing you is so crippling that I can barely hold pieces of myself together. The slightest nudge could break me. But somehow, my possessed brain knows what I need. It's telling me to stick to my choice, to stay away from you, to open a Word document and bleed on paper, try to throw up all my jumbled thoughts in form of words, collect all disconnected facts, try to make sense of it all.' From the bestselling author of *Like a Love Song* and *Every Time It Rains*, a story of heartbreak and things left unsaid ...

Siddhant meets Akriti during their medical residency in Delhi. Their connection is instant, blossoming from the many similarities between them. So, when Akriti faces a devastating loss, she leans on Siddhant for support. In the heat of an emotional moment, the two decide that this must be love. But as Akriti's depression begins to take a stronger hold over her, she spirals out of control, sinking deeper into an abyss of fear, insecurity and rage. And while Siddhant struggles to help her, it seems like everything he does is only making things worse. Meanwhile, Siddhant's life gets further complicated when Maahi, his ex-girlfriend whom he never stopped loving, re-enters his life.Nikita Singh returns with a stirring story – exploring emotional health, the boundaries of traditional relationships and second chances.